The Art of Growing Old

A Guide to Faithful Aging

THE

Art

OF GROWING OLD

CARROLL SAUSSY

Augsburg
MINNEAPOLIS

THE ART OF GROWING OLD
A Guide to Faithful Aging

Book and cover design by Joseph Bonyata

Library of Congress Cataloging-in-Publication-Data

Saussy, Carroll
    The art of growing old : a guide to faithful aging / Carroll
    Saussy
        p.   cm.
    Includes bibliographical references.
    ISBN 0-8066-3617-3 (alk. paper)
    1. Aging—Psychological aspects—United States. 2. Life change events in old age—United States. 3. Self-perception in old-age—United States. 4. Self-esteem in old age—United States.
    I. Title.
HQ1064.U5S295   1998
305.26'0973—dc21   98-11217
                                                                    CIP

The paper used in this publication meets the minimum requirements of American National Standards for Information Sciences—Permanence of Paper for Printed Library Materials, ANSI Z329.48-1984.   ∞

Manufactured in the U.S.A.   AF9-3617

04   03   02   01   3   4   5   6   7

Dedicated to
Frank Armstrong Molony
wise and wonderful partner in faithful aging

Contents

Acknowledgments

M Y THANKS GO TO SO MANY COLLEAGUES who encouraged this work on aging. I am especially grateful to my husband Frank Molony, who not only read the manuscript but found himself in its pages and kept the conversation going all year about much of the content. I am grateful to research librarian Howertine Duncan and inspiring friend Mary Hunt who faithfully fed me books and titles; thanks to Rollie Radloff and Jim Weaver, colleagues in faithful aging who provided encouraging feedback on the manuscript; thanks to Cynthia Thompson, who believed in the value of my book from the start and gently pushed me to strengthen it; and thanks to Ron Klug for wise and witty editorial advice. Finally, I am grateful to Wesley Theological Seminary for a full-year sabbatical during which I increased with delight in knowledge and age and wisdom.

Introduction

Thinking Age

I want to tell people approaching and perhaps fearing age that it is a time of discovery. If they say—"Of what?" I can only answer, "We must each find out for ourselves."

—*Florida Scott-Maxwell*, The Measure of My Days

As MY SIXTIETH BIRTHDAY APPROACHED, I reflected on a teaching experience twenty years earlier. Nursing students enrolled in a course entitled "The Mystery of Suffering and Death" began the semester by reading psychiatrist Virginia Axline's remarkable account of play therapy with six-year-old Dibs. Believed by his parents to be autistic, Dibs was in fact a bright but unwanted child who refused to speak.

Prior to plunging into a discussion of the book, *Dibs In Search of Self*, I asked the students to take a ten-minute walk on the colorful fall campus and "think six." I wanted them to be able to walk in Dibs's shoes when they discussed the book and assumed that their experience at six would be dramatically different from his. Later in the semester, after students read Elisabeth Kübler-Ross, *On Death and Dying*, their exercise was a walk "thinking sixty." The results of these two excursions were quite amazing.

"Think six" brought back fear, insecurity, the anxiety over separation from parents and home. I had anticipated memories of wonder, delight, and carefree days—backyard and playground and neighborhood fun, but painful memories returned to students in their twenties who relived their first day of school.

In contrast, students returned from their "think sixty" stroll not with apprehension of nursing homes or aging minds and bodies but aglow with thoughts of grandmothering healthy grandchildren, baking cookies, telling stories, and initiating exotic travel adventures with vigorous spouses. Both then and now, their reflections conjure up for me a gray woman, hair twisted into a bun, apron covering her house dress. Standing at the kitchen counter with a large, pleasant smile on her well-lined face, she doesn't look like any sixty-year-old I know today.

As I recall that day in class, concerns about aging or ill health, loss or insecurity were not part of the nursing students' reflections. Granted, these were largely middle-class white women, recently out of high school and soon ready to launch their first careers. For them, thinking sixty bordered on the ridiculous.

The senior person in the room, I was too far into adulthood to share their idyllic fantasies of sixty. For me, sixty *did* have the feel of genuine old age; not yet forty, I could easily keep sixty at a safe distance. (Now past sixty, I feel "old age" doesn't include me yet, but refers to people in their mid-eighties.) The students were too young to let the predictable losses of old age cloud their dreams. I did anticipate clouds, unaware at the time that the serious losses in old age most often come much later than sixty. I was a generation away from sixty. The students were "lifetimes" away.

One reason aging sneaks up on most people is that prior

to midlife, people have an enormous capacity to deny the fact that the young are in many ways very much like the old, sharing the same basic wants and needs. The young, like the old, are aging with each passing day. Aging doesn't start at a certain moment in the life cycle or belong exclusively to an unfortunate, isolated group of ancient people. It is always now and belongs to everyone.

Hear an exchange between age and young adulthood in Louis De Bernieres's novel, *Corelli's Mandolin*. Deciding against having children, Antonia and Alexi spent the first years of marriage building their fortune. Antonia's adopted mother, Pelagia, has been unsuccessful in her repeated attempts to coax her daughter into producing a grandchild. Four years "after her womb began to clamour for an occupant," Antonia forgot to take her birth control pill. Pelagia, delighted to learn of the pregnancy, is eager to name the child.

> "I'm an old woman," declared Pelagia, who gained substantial gratification from reiterating this refrain. "It might be my last wish."
> "You're sixty. These days that isn't old."
> "Well, I feel old."
> "Well, you don't look it."
> "I didn't bring you up to be a liar," said Pelagia, terribly pleased nonetheless.
> "I'm thirty-four," said Antonia, "that's old. Sixty is just a number."[1]

In other words, Antonia belongs to a different subspecies than Pelagia, a class that measures its years by special calendars. The two subgroups remain distinct.

My research on aging began as a self-imposed assignment. Well aware that sixty is more than a number, I chose to exercise a modest measure of control over my own life cycle. I have no illusions of either stopping the clock or going back a few decades. Rather I seek wisdom about how to move into the last decades of life with a sense of expectation, grace, and fulfillment. Grace is used here theologically to refer to the action of God's Spirit within, luring human beings to live as fully and generatively as possible.

Reflective Pause

At points in this book I ask you, the reader, to reflect on an issue or question before reading further. I strongly recommend that you keep notes about these reflections, as well as written responses to questions and suggestions at the end of the chapters and any other writing that springs from your thoughts on aging. All of your jottings will be useful to the work of the final chapter, and, I hope, to your journey into age.

Spend a few moments imagining yourself arising on the morning of your sixtieth birthday. For some readers this will require looking back; for others, anticipating. How do you or did you feel about your birthday? How would you describe your hopes, your fears, your attitude at sixty?

Next, think eighty. Imagine your eightieth birthday party. Who will be there? What will you look like? For octogenarians, who was there? Again, consider your hopes and fears and attitude. Finally, leap ahead one decade and think ninety, asking yourself the same questions.

Chronological Stages of Adult Life

When does genuine old age begin? When you think about your own aging, how far into the future can you sustain the reflection? About midway in my research for this book, I realized that I had mostly the sixties and seventies in mind when I set out to study aging. Already sixty, my ageist thinking pushed my own timeline forward twenty years; however, I did not want to reflect much beyond eighty.[2]

When is one old? Dividing the adult life cycle into age segments is not easy. When Erik Erikson wrote *Childhood and Society* in 1950, he believed that adolescence ended at eighteen, young adulthood at thirty, and that old age began at fifty-five. When Gail Sheehy wrote her first *Passages* in 1976, she saw the mid-thirties as the prime of life, the halfway mark signaling that the parabola had reversed. Sheehy stopped at fifty, she reveals nearly twenty years later in *New Passages*, because she was unable to imagine either herself at that age or life beyond fifty. Now Sheehy holds that adulthood begins at thirty, and that middle adulthood does not begin until the fifties.

There are at least three reasons why it is difficult to categorize people according to chronological stages. First, norms for what one calls childhood, adolescence, adulthood, and old age are always shifting. Second, increased longevity lengthens the period that has been called old age to one third, and for some as much as one half, of a normal lifetime—too long an epoch to be considered one stage. Third, it is difficult for writers to project themselves into anything more than their immediate futures; they simply lack firsthand experience, and their imaginations fail.

1. *Shifting norms.* Erik Erikson was well aware of the sociological shift of norms for adolescence during the twenty five years after publication of *Childhood and Society*. In conversation with a group of doctoral students from the Graduate Theological Union in Berkeley in 1976, Erikson was asked what chronological age he might assign to adolescence. He could not give a precise answer, saying that in

this country adolescence might end somewhere around thirty.

In recent decades adult ages have shifted approximately ten years. In other words, a fifty-year old resembles what used to be seen at age forty. A sixty-year old today is physically and emotionally more like the fifty-year old of a generation ago. At seventy people resemble their parents at sixty. Will medical advances, good health habits, and evolving socialization keep pushing back the horizon of aging bodies and psyches?

2. *Increased longevity.* Current average life expectancy for persons who have reached sixty-five is eighty-two. For women, old age is often longer. In 1994, elderly women outnumbered older men by a ratio of three to two; the ratio reaches five to two in the population over eighty-five.[3] The numbers of centenarians in the United States totaled 37,000 in 1990; by the year 2000, the figure will pass 100,000.[4]

The challenge remains to divide a long span of years called old age into subcategories.

3. *Projecting oneself into old age.* The final reason it is difficult to assign labels to chronological ages or stages is because writers have a hard time fully projecting themselves into their future. At forty, I saw sixty as quite old. At sixty, I have a hard time claiming that I am even "young old." People in their seventies and eighties mock me in a friendly sort of way when I say I am old. To them sixty-two is "a piece of cake."

Faced with the dilemma of writing about late adult life without well-defined markers, I follow roughly the three categories suggested by the National Council on the Aging: young-old (60-75), middle-old (75-85), and old-old (85+).

When speaking about the old in general, I use *old age* and *elders* of persons who are sixty and older. Because sixty and older covers a span of more than thirty years, generalizations about old age are difficult. No doubt, many readers will find statements in this book that do not match their experience, but although generalizations are dangerous, they make it possible to recognize patterns and discover possibilities.

Theories of Aging

The confusion around aging norms and expectations shows up in theories that attempt to explain social activity in old age.

Activity Theory

According to *activity theory*, the decrease in social activity of older people is the result of society's withdrawal from the aging person. With basically the same psychological and social needs they experienced in middle age, older people do not welcome the change in society's attitudes. They want to maintain the level of engagement that they pursued in middle age.[5]

Disengagement Theory

Disengagement theory holds that both society and the aging person willingly withdraw from each other. The old person seeks less social interaction; social groups and institutions offer fewer possibilities. The pulling away is mutual.

Some social psychologists believe that old persons both regret and accept the drop in role activity they experience as they age. The same old person both wants to stay active and engaged with others, and desires to withdraw and pursue a more leisurely or more contemplative way of life. There are elders who succeed in maintaining a sense of self-worth and satisfaction in their lives through the change. Others are less successful in maintaining self-esteem and are dissatisfied.[6]

Continuity Theory

Finally, the *continuity theory* of aging stresses that people age as they have lived. Some seek far more social interaction than others. Old people want gradual change that allows both for consistency and novelty.[7]

The Baltimore Longitudinal Study of Aging basically supports the continuity theory in the aging process of healthy people. Initiated by Dr. Nathan Shock and the National Institutes of Health in 1958 and turned over to the National Institute of Aging in 1975, the biomedical and psychological study has sought to understand normal aging. More than 2,400 volunteers from their twenties through their nineties have participated. All are community-dwelling volunteers who are followed through their lifetimes.

Several findings of researchers underscore continuity throughout adulthood. First, the personality of mentally healthy adults remains steady throughout the adult years. Aging is highly individual, highly specific for both the individual and for the various organ systems within each individual. In other words, difficult, unhappy young adults become difficult, unhappy old adults. Researchers suggest that the fundamental question of aging needs recasting. Do not ask how aging changes personality; ask how enduring personality traits fashion a whole life.

Second, in terms of loss and decline of bodily and mental functions, the findings offer no major surprises. Many physical and mental functions gradually but steadily decline. At the same time, many mental capacities remain constant. Vocabulary continues to increase and analytical and problem-solving skills are retained. While memory may decline and the brain take more time to make decisions, there is ample brain capacity in reserve. Illness is more significant than age in bringing about decline. Sudden changes are an expression of disease or closely related to disease, not the result of aging itself.

Compensatory changes are the body and mind's way of maintaining continuous function. An old heart cannot increase its pumping rate, but it dilates to a greater extent and pumps more blood with each heart beat. Memory declines, but knowledge may increase. Finally, changes in diet and exercise, part of cultural awareness of healthy living, help maintain a high quality of life for older adults.[8]

Growing Old

This book is for all adults interested in increasing satisfaction in their lives. It gives an overview of aging, with an emphasis on the tasks that aging persons in this country face as they enter into and proceed through the last quarter of their lives. The book provides practical ways in which these tasks might be accomplished. You will be encouraged frequently to face your own life cycle with a view toward aging. I hope that the reflections and questions raised in these pages will provide challenge, excitement, playfulness, and a sense of the absurd for people who want to enjoy life to the end. Aging belongs to everyone. If all adults faced up to their one and only life cycle, they might find creative, shared ways of living and aging among one another, that is, with adults of all ages. Thus one of the most serious problems of old age, social isolation, might be resolved.

I bring a passionate interest in religious faith to this topic, convinced that spirituality and contemplation are invaluable tools for faithful aging, and that churches and synagogues are ideal places where faithful aging can be fostered. I hope this book is a useful tool for clergy, lay leaders, and members of congregations interested in effective work among adults, specifically with elders.

Not many years from retirement, I bring a personal agenda to this project as well. Convinced that old age should be a time of renaissance and new beginnings, a time to awaken sleeping possibilities, I want to shape a new ministry with older members of congregations as they face the realities of age and move into their futures. I also want to work with congregations in developing intergenerational ministries.

The goal of this book is to support adults of all ages in rediscovering themselves within the relationships, activities, and values that constitute their lives. It is especially to support elders, to assist them in truly *growing* old, not simply aging.

Chapter 1 invites you to face up to your one and only life cycle. This requires coming to terms with the universal fact of mortality, beginning with your own, as well as finding effective ways of living in the present moment. Faithful aging happens hour by hour, day by day.

Chapter 2 explores the reality of loss throughout life and suggests ways of living successfully with it. Losses overlap within networks of change: the loss of material possessions, physical and bodily loss, psychological and spiritual loss, relational loss, and role loss are discussed, especially as these occur in the last quarter of life.

In chapter 3 the negative attitudes and stereotypes projected onto elders are explored and rejected. In their place, new images of aging are suggested. Everyone must face the reality of age. No one, however, is encouraged to accept the negative stereotypes of aging that abound.

Past, present, and future all shape the quality of present life. The past lives in the present; the future springs from the present. The first three chapters focus mainly on the present. The next tasks of aging are related to the past and the future.

Chapter 4 considers how the past influences the present, both in positive and negative ways. Our task is to devise a more usable past. Acquiring a usable past involves rediscovering gifts and values that have been sleeping. Finding a usable past also involves remembering, reframing, sometimes forgiving, and surrendering feelings of disappointment and loss. I was challenged by an Austrian historian with whom I discussed the concept of a usable past. He explained that many Germans and Austrians who were part of Hitler's regime devised a usable past by rewriting history in a way that made it possible for them to live more comfortably with themselves. They feel vindicated by the distorted revisions. What I mean by finding a usable past is quite the opposite. One sustains an *honest* confrontation with the past for the sake of living with renewed purpose and an enlightened sense of self, solidly rooted in one's history.

Chapter 5 turns to the future. Human life requires hope and a sense of future. As people age, their hopes and expectations of the future evolve. Changed living circumstances, technological advances, health issues, religious experience, the death or moves of significant persons in their lives can bring an end to some dreams and open the way for other possibilities. The future contains only possibilities—possibilities that need to be named and claimed as one chooses maps, marks routes, and plans the future journey.

The final task is to return to the present, enriched by a reclaimed past and with a future story in mind. Chapter 6 helps the reader create a more engaging and faithful present. By an exploration of the values that you have cherished, you will find ways either to realize these values in the present or to pursue new values that better match your current way of life.

In chapter 7 you will be asked to outline a brief story of your life as a way of pulling together the work of the book and concluding—for now. The task of faithful aging, of course, goes on with the steady beat of time. I intend to write a sequel to this book in ten years; that plan is an integral part of *my* future story.

Each chapter moves from theory to practice, with suggestions and illustrations of how the various tasks of aging might be accomplished. Although gaining knowledge of new possibilities may be the beginning of change, the actual transformation of a life occurs when we set goals, make plans, and enact those plans. A massive study of self-esteem conducted by a team of psychologists came to a single major conclusion. People have high self-esteem when they do something about perceived problems in their lives. They have low self-esteem when they avoid these issues.[9] People age faithfully when they take charge of their elder years, rising to the challenges of old age; they age with regrets when they passively let the years slip by.

Suggestions and questions at the end of each chapter provide a variety of ways in which you can move toward accomplishing the tasks of aging outlined in this book. Although you may not choose to complete all the suggested activities, I strongly encourage you to spend time on some of the exercises in each chapter.

Following the exercises in each chapter is a guided meditation, offered as a way of reflecting prayerfully on the topic at hand. Some people will find it difficult to read and engage in the meditation at the same time. One way to alleviate the problem is to make a tape recording of the meditations, leaving long enough pauses at the dots to allow for reflection. Another possibility is to recruit another person to read the meditation or to agree with another to work through the book together, each taking turns in reading the meditation for the other.

While individual readers can gain insight and effect change through applying the exercises and completing the meditations on their own, the work of this book may be accomplished best within an ongoing group. The possibilities are many: women's groups, men's groups, mixed groups, neighborhood groups, social groups. For persons rooted in religious faith, a church-based group could provide an ideal setting for engaging in faithful aging. Hopefully, people with a common faith in God are free to share with one another their hopes and doubts, their values and their concerns, and support one another as they dream new dreams. (Suggestions for the make-up of groups and guidelines for group facilitators are found in the appendices.)

Some readers may resist focusing on their own journeys of faith and aging. Admittedly, a good bit of the attention in this book is on the self, but the focus is also on the family from which you came, the family in which you are presently rooted, and the community in which you live. Community is central to the work of faithful aging; more genuine community is desired, a community that is justice-seeking, sensitive, generative, and neighborly. The design of the book includes self-focus, not self-indulgence. Like most good things, self-reflection can become an obsessive preoccupation. That is not what I intend. The goal of the exercises is the enjoyment of richer and more generative relationships to others, to one's community, and to God.

Faithful aging is *growing* old, embracing not only the more painful challenges of a long life, but engaging the possibilities for creativity and depth of soul available to those who have acquired a wealth of experience. New prospects that come with the availability of time, wisdom gained through lived experience, and individual gifts and talents— these are the resources for faithful aging.

1

Facing Up to Your Life Cycle

We must seriously enter into the experience of the sands slip-
ping away in the hourglass of our lives. This discomforting feel-
ing of the unstoppable dimming of the light, the numbering of
breaths, must be embraced until it hurts.

　　　　　　　—*Eugene Bianchi,* Aging as a Spiritual Journey

MANY PEOPLE WANT TO LIVE TO A ripe old age, especially when they consider the alternative. Some want the
impossible: they want to live long, but they don't want to get
old. How many people over fifty are willing to seriously face
the realities of age in order to age faithfully?

This chapter considers two realities which, when faced,
can enhance the life and growth of elders. First is the fact of
mortality: the inevitability of death must be looked at head
on, "embraced until it hurts." Second is the fact that all anyone has at her or his disposal is the present moment. Both
past and future are profoundly important to an individual's
journey, but the past is available only in memory, and the
future, only in possibility. Faithful aging happens in the present. The advantages of living in the present moment are
explored in the second part of the chapter.

The Human Condition: Mortality

Facing age head on means affirming the reality of death. While some people are far more successful than others in avoiding the fact that all human beings die, the desire to evade facing death is strong and deep in the human psyche.

Stop, look, and listen to the world around you. Why the glorification of youth? Why the frequent isolation of elders "with their own kind," rather than their integration into intergenerational communities? Age is a reminder of death, and most people want to keep the thought of death at bay. While people may not be able to avoid facing the death of others, they can attempt to live as if they are somehow spared such a fate themselves.

In the early stages of human development, the brevity of life can be more successfully denied. Children can't wait to reach the next birthday, giving no thought to the number of years that might or might not lie beyond this year's candles. Adolescents see the future as happening at eighteen or twenty-one. For them, looking beyond twenty-one stirs anxiety. Although there will still be *some* years left, there won't be many, they think, because for them old age begins at thirty. The actual dread of the young is that they will not be seen as young by the young. They fear crossing the artificial barrier that separates them from belonging to the in-crowd, an exclusive privilege of the young. Real old age is for the unfortunates; real old age is far beyond youth's worrying about. Thirty-four is old, Antonia told Pelagia, "Sixty is just a number."

The vast majority of people over fifty are in the second half of their lives; they have lived longer than they will live, and as birthdays approach, they tend to think of years left rather than years spent. Denial of mortality is such a pervasive human behavior, however, that many may reflect only fleetingly on years left when they "celebrate" birthdays after fifty, yielding to empty slogans such as, "You're not getting older, you're getting better," "You're only as old as you feel," and "You haven't changed a bit." The hard truth is that every living person is always getting older. There are both feel-good and feel-bad days throughout a human lifetime, and many people, who are in fact always changing, may well be much older than they look or feel.

When I had just quietly slipped through my fortieth birthday, a colleague gave me social psychologist Ernest Becker's new book, *The Denial of Death.* Could Becker possibly be right, I asked myself, in claiming that the fundamental drive in human life is to deny death? Although I did not agree with Becker that human beings seek to be *heroic* in order to rise above the human condition, I was convinced that on at least two counts he was right. First, the denial of death, which I believe to be secondary to the primary drive to survive and thrive, is pervasive; second, the need to be in control can be an attempt to deny limits. (Sometimes the need for control grows out of a person or group's experience of having been dominated and oppressed by others. The need for control can express both a survival and a justice need, not denying limits but affirming possibilities.)

More than twenty years later I am still persuaded that the denial of death and the avoidance of age are serious issues that can reduce the quality of life for young and old alike. Old people remind younger adults that they have given insufficient attention to their own inevitable mortality. A primary reason younger people avoid or isolate the aging, and divert their eyes from the eyes of older persons, is that lined faces and aging bodies are too strong an intimation of mortality.

Drawing back from old people could result from fear that the old possess some power to pull the no-longer-young down under with them. This repulsion shows up in hospitals and geriatric institutions, on the part of both the young and the middle-aged. Author Ronald Blythe sees people of all ages positioning themselves apart from the old. The middle-aged's repulsion covers a tough shield that protects them from facing their own limits. They feel more vulnerable in the presence of the old and offer their compassion at arm's length. Young doctors and nurses cannot conceive that what they witness among their patients will ever be their fate. Youth serving on a geriatric ward feel super healthy next to the deteriorating health of the elderly.[1]

One way the young avoid their inevitable aging is to look at the old and see the past, but fail to see their own future. In turn, aging persons in denial can look at the young and see their own past but are disinclined to look into the future of the young, because in doing so they must see beyond their own life cycle. Many older old *do* see beyond their own life cycle and come to speak readily of their sure demise.

In an age of AIDS, increased violence against women and children, an epidemic of street violence and terrorism, airplane disasters, and wars in many corners of the globe, perhaps the whole world faces death with far greater frequency and intensity than in the 1970s when Becker wrote *The Denial of Death*. "It *will* happen to me" may be more readily acknowledged.

The denial of death may not be as prevalent in ethnic communities that have lived within a hostile majority society, with little sense of security beyond their own walls. Pastoral theologian Teresa Snorton believes that African Americans, with wide eyes and without a tremble, are able to stare into the face of death.[2]

Women of all races, inhabitants of an often hostile male-dominated society, may deny death less than the dominant group—in this country, European-American males. In her cross-cultural research among women forty-five and older, religious educator Maria Harris found women to be generally excited about their aging process, giving little evidence of the fear or denial of death.[3] There was a time when the fear of death was more prevalent at the beginning of life than in its last quarter. When child mortality was high, the fear of death on the part of parents and the reality of death in childhood were very present threats: the cradle was all too close to the grave.[4] To survive birth and infancy, then childhood, was to *live*. The old could feel distanced from death by the fact that they made it through childhood.

Even if one accepts that death is certainly in the future, however, it is not easy to talk about this universal fact in most circles. Talk about death is considered morbid. A resident in a private retirement home in Birmingham, Alabama, asked me what brought me there. I explained that I was writing a book on aging. "There are 148 guinea pigs here," she said laughing. "You'll have to stay over." When asked if residents talked about their experience of getting old, she replied, "No, we don't have serious conversations in here. We have only superficial conversations." Even the retirees in a nursing home can be adept at keeping their concerns of aging and death at bay. In general the old are not encouraged to discuss death except perhaps with a few close family members and friends, well-trained ministers, and medical or hospice professionals.

When my sister's mother-in-law was suffering progressive memory loss, she wandered into a group of my women colleagues who were having a meeting in the shade of a tree in Louisiana.[5] She had gotten into the habit of walking out of her home two miles down the road, being picked up by someone in the small town who knew that she was headed to her son's house, and then delivered to his driveway. This day she saw women gathered in the backyard and came to join what looked like a party. After I introduced her to my colleagues and explained what the meeting was about, Granny brought up her memory problem.

"They don't like me walking over, and they worry because I forget things." After a few exchanges among us and an awkward silence as I tried to figure out how to handle the situation, she leaned forward and asked, "Would you do me a favor? When they are my age [presumably, when my brother-in-law and sister were in their seventies], would you let me know how well they remember?" Then she caught herself and chuckled. "I might not be around . . . I suppose I won't, but I would love to know and I wish you could tell me. Tell me if you can." I can see still the passion in her eyes. I had not witnessed someone surprise herself by facing the reality of death in midsentence. Granny was thinking beyond her days and had to cut herself out of the picture at the same time that she wanted very much to be in the picture.

Facing death head-on requires serious and sometimes sustained reflection. Theologian Eugene Bianchi's words at the opening of this chapter echo Ernest Becker. The sands are slipping away: one's breaths are numbered. The reality of death must be embraced until it hurts. Then comes the freedom for passionate living into the limited but inviting future.

Affirming the inevitability of death does not mean that old people need to make death a central or everyday thought or conversation topic. Facing death does not require dwelling on death. People can talk about aging, about how they want to live before they die, without overfocusing on their inevitable deaths.

Usually the thought of death is kept at a distance, and well it might be. The denial of death is a useful strategy that enables mortal human beings to move into the future with energy, hope, and dreams. Becker believed that strategies for keeping death at bay serve people well once they have truly faced the fact of mortality—without blinking, diverting their eyes, or hiding behind dark glasses.

To bring home this point, when I teach a course on dying, death, and bereavement, I have students say out loud with me, "One day I will no longer walk upon the earth." It is a sobering experience. We also look around the room and reflect on the fact that in fewer than one hundred years not one of us will be alive.

A central way of facing the reality of limits is to come to terms with one's life cycle. Once people accept their life cycle as their one and only life cycle, psychologist Erik Erikson has taught us, they can achieve a sense of integrity, and with it, wisdom. Faithful aging requires that people be true to themselves. They can be true to themselves only if they are able to face who they are: limited, finite creatures who will die. Having accepted the ultimate loss that is surely in their future, they can more gracefully deal with the intermediate losses that are indeed a part of everyday life and they can live more passionately in the present.

Living in the Present Moment

When I reflect on the meaning of the present, my imagination flies back to a period in young adulthood when I was guided into the contemplative life and introduced to the concept of "living in the present moment." The world stood still as in awe and wonder I felt endless possibility in fully attending to the *now.* Several specific memories flood my imagination. Some of them are nature-based experiences of being suspended in amazed contemplation of the plant world, bathing in the wonder of leaf and tree and sky. Bird watching, too, became an awesome experience. Other memorable moments are mind-focused and heart-filled times of silent prayer, wordless contemplation of the reality of being, the miracle of life. Biblical passages offered fresh messages of God's boundless love and ceaseless caring. Learning to live in the present moment meant suspending distractions and focusing my very active imagination, keeping worries at bay, relishing the now, and so often enjoying an awareness of divine presence.

The only moment anyone has is indeed the present moment. The past, though gone, lives in the present. The future, nothing but possibilities, is not yet present. I have this moment, only this moment.

The ability to live with others in the present moment can greatly enhance one's capacity for genuine relationship. How rare it is when people manage to relinquish their own agenda and fully attend to another person. This takes the same kind of discipline I learned in developing a prayer life. Living in the present moment is a sure way to enhance your life and the relationships that enrich it, because in the present moment you can become aware of the beauty of the other.

Thomas Merton's recounting of a mystical experience he enjoyed on a bustling street in Louisville illustrates what the present moment, fully attended to, can reveal. Merton was at a busy corner in the center of the shopping district when he suddenly realized that he loved all the people around him. They were his, and he was theirs. He knew that they could not be aliens to one another, although they were total strangers. Merton said he almost laughed out loud. He was overwhelmed by the immense joy of belonging to the human race in which God became incarnate. He had to hold back from blurting out to people how he saw them: they were all "walking around shining like the sun."[6]

The present as season. In everyday language, the present refers not so much to the prevailing moment in time, but to the current season or period of one's life. Seasons are marked, if not by natural rhythm of summer, fall, winter, and spring, then by life periods punctuated by such events as job change, relocation of home, births and deaths, and other milestones in family life. Attending to the present season in your life requires that you take stock of how your life is being lived and enjoyed, or simply sustained and tolerated, in order for you to make changes that will increase its quality. Attending to the present moment is an intense way of getting to the heart of the matter.

"For everything there is a season, and a time for every matter under heaven" (Ecclesiastes 3:1). There is a time to be young, and for those who are lucky, a time to grow old. If there is indeed a season for everything under the sun, then old age has its unique promises and possibilities—its unique season, its *kairos*.

Kairos, peaks, plateaus, and growing old. The Greek word *kairos* designates the fullness of time, different from *chronos*, a particular hour or day in chronological time. *Kairos* is the time of salvation; it cannot be controlled by human intervention. Biblical *kairos* primarily refers to the coming, dying, and rising of Jesus, salvation events that brought a new world of possibilities to humankind. Every moment is potentially *kairos*, available to the person who faithfully meets the challenge of life in God's universe and experiences salvation (see Romans 13:11; Galatians 6:9-10). Faithful aging means rising to the challenge in this *kairos*, using the possibilities of the moment, seeing through chronological time and into God's time.

Psychological literature describes similar experiences of the fullness of the present moment. An acknowledged agnostic, humanistic psychologist Abraham Maslow called such flashes of enlarged awareness *peak experiences.* In a peak experience a person feels integrated, more fully functioning, and at the same time more able to fuse or become one with another or with the world. Fear and inhibitions disappear, and the person feels more spontaneous, self-expressive, and renewed.[7] Something new is indeed present: a new awareness, a revelation, a desire to yield to the goodness of life. Revelatory experiences that last for more than a few moments are *plateau experiences.* Living on a plateau, one encounters life with new eyes and ears and heart, and renewed imagination. In both peak experiences and plateau experiences, you perceive the world as a whole and yourself at a profound level, at the level of soul. Living on a high plateau is achieved when you learn how to discover the sacred in the ordinary. While the peak experience is essentially emotional, the plateau experience is essentially cognitive. For one who believes in God, peaks and plateaus are filled with divine grace.

I am not suggesting that anyone can sail through old age on a heightened plateau. I do believe, however, that accepting the challenge of aging faithfully and boldly embracing this new era with anticipation and focused attention, brings a person close to peaks or plateaus and to the enjoyment of *kairos.* Every moment is *chronos,* a segment of clock time. Every moment is potentially *kairos,* a glimmer of the eternal.

Conclusion

There is an obvious connection between fully living in the present moment and wholly accepting the human condition. The present moment is the place where a person is who and what she is and no one else. She is a limited human being with real possibilities and limitations. As persons come to a more mature and deeper self-knowledge, they gain a facility for stepping outside themselves and seeing the whole, entering with greater ease into the present moment.

Mortal and finite, every living human being has only the present moment in which to grow old faithfully. The ultimate loss will be death. Along the way, there are multiple losses with which one must live and grow. Living with loss is the topic of chapter 2.

For Personal Reflection

1. How were you introduced to death as a child? What was your first actual experience of death? How was the death handled within your family?

2. Recall your first viewing of a dead person and your first funeral. What feelings come up for you?

3. What is the most significant death you have experienced? How does the loss still live in you?

4. Think about your own death. How old do you want to be when you die? What kind of funeral or memorial service would you want held for you? Write your own epitaph and share it with someone close to you.

5. Spend five minutes opening yourself to the present moment in whatever way you feel drawn. You might use a word or brief special phrase that centers your imagination and brings you home to yourself. After your five-minute

reflection, move to the meditation that concludes this chapter.

Meditation

This is the first of the guided meditations. If you are using this book in group discussion, see the guidelines for facilitating meditations in Appendix C. If you are making the meditation on your own, begin by finding a comfortable chair in a quiet place where you will not be disturbed. You may choose to light a candle or in some other way prepare your space. Such things as a fragrance, soothing music, a bowl of flowers or fruit or vegetables, a photograph or art object can enhance your sense of the sacred in your space.

With your feet on the floor and your arms and hands at rest, take three deep breaths as you let go of distractions. Relax your body from head to foot, and come home to yourself. If you feel stress in any part of your body, focus on that body part. Tighten the muscles in the tense part of the body, hold onto the tension for a few seconds, then totally relax. When you feel relaxed and ready, either play the tape recording you have made of the meditation or slowly read it, pausing at the dots to reflect on what has just been suggested to you. Closing your eyes during the pauses might help you stay focused and to follow the lead of your imagination. At the end of the meditation, take time to come back to everyday consciousness. You might make notes about your experience.

I am about to do a new thing; now it springs forth,
do you not perceive it? (Isaiah 43:19).

Go to a place that has given you great satisfaction during a spring season in your past, a place that calms your soul and feasts your eyes. Breathe in the fresh, fragrant spring air. . . . Note the color of the sky, the spring flowers in bud. . . . Listen for the sound of birds, the splash of water in fountain or stream. Settle down and enjoy the peace, the stillness, your inner calm.

> *I am about to do a new thing; now it springs forth,*
> *do you not perceive it?*

You are alone, peaceful, relaxed. There are benches if you wish to sit down, paths if you want to walk. . . . As you become very calm, very quiet, happy to be where you are, you are aware of a presence. A wise old person you have known in a mutually trusting relationship walks toward you. You greet each other, embrace, and begin a conversation. . . . What do you want to say? What do you want to hear? . . .

You become powerfully aware of the presence of the Holy One in your midst. It is as if time stands still—two caring people reaching out to one another. What do you want to say? What do you want to hear? . . .

> *I am about to do a new thing; now it springs forth,*
> *do you not perceive it?*

What is the new thing happening here? . . . As you prepare to say good-bye to one another, you realize that indeed you are the wise old one; a younger person in your life is meeting you in the future. Stay with this change for a few moments. Get comfortably calm. Come home to yourself. What do you want to say? What do you want to hear? . . .

Share some of your thoughts and anxieties about

aging. . . . Speak about your hopes for the future. . . . Once again, you are vividly aware of God's presence in your life, in your hopes, in your dreams, in your relationships. Your friend tells you how much you have meant to him or her; you express what this relationship means to you, especially now that you are old. . . . What wisdom do you want to share with your friend?

Talk about when you will see each other again as you express your pleasure and your gratitude and prepare to depart. . . . In a moment of silence, the two of you look around, look at one another, embrace, and go your separate ways. . . .

Aware of the holy, let yourself become one with the "I" as you hear:

We are about to do a new thing; now it springs forth,
do you not perceive it? Blessed be.

Further Reflection

If the meditation worked, you crossed a bridge back into the past, then moved forward. For some this involved past and future; for others, past and present. What did you learn about how you perceive and live with the realities of age? Were you aware of stereotypes—either experiencing them or replacing them? Did you discover new understanding about living in the present moment? You may want to write your responses in your journal or share them with a friend or small group.

2

Living with Loss

It is our attitude toward our losses as much as the nature of our losses which will determine the quality of our old age.
— Judith Viorst, Necessary Losses

THE OLD DO NOT HAVE A CORNER ON LOSS. Loss is a part of life from birth through death, and attitudes toward loss go as far back as each individual's birth. Living well with loss means finding some gain in the process of letting go. One value is replaced by another value. The person suffering loss discovers that life is meaningful nevertheless.

The newborn child must lose its prenatal environment in order to become a separate person. The toddler gives up the bottle and drinks from a cup. The kindergartner surrenders some of the freedom of a less structured play world and faces the limits and possibilities of organized learning and play. Early in life the gains surely outweigh what has been left behind.

With age, however, the gains may become more ambiguous. Moving into adolescence ends a far more carefree and less self-conscious period of development. Not all girls and boys entering puberty are eager to let go of childhood. Relinquishing status as high school seniors to become lowly college freshmen is a mixed blessing. Giving up college life to enter the career world means a complex of losses and gains, experienced quite differently from person to person. A first full-time job, with two weeks vacation after fifty weeks of employment, comes as a shock to many young adults. Newlywed couples might disagree among themselves and within a single relationship about the losses and gains of married life. Gay and lesbian youth and adults know intense loss and gain when publicly they claim their sexuality. Parents could dispute the various losses and gains of the empty nest. Retirees would not speak with one mind on the losses and gains of ending one's career.

While *attitude* toward loss may be as significant as the *nature* of the loss in determining quality of life, attitude toward loss is shaped largely by several variables that govern the way a loss is felt. These include whether the loss is avoidable or unavoidable, temporary or permanent, actual or imagined, anticipated or unanticipated, and whether a person is leaving or being left.[1]

An avoidable loss will be felt more acutely and with a sense of guilt and regret that an unavoidable loss may not entail. Old people eventually die; their death is unavoidable. The loss of life due to street violence or drunk driving could be avoided—not that a victim has the power to avoid the gun or head-on collision. When people blame themselves for the loss of health, the loss of a job, the loss of an election, the loss of a relationship, particularly of a marriage, gnawing guilt makes it difficult for them to let go and move on.

The temporary loss of a friend or role is easier to live with than a permanent or irreversible loss.

Often imagined losses can be dealt with through a good conversation with a wise friend or therapist; actual losses are not as readily sustained.

An anticipated loss is far easier to face than a sudden, shocking loss.

The person freely making the decision to leave a relationship or an institution will have a different and usually less painful emotional journey to make than the person being left behind.

A good starting place in exploring loss in old age is to recognize that a loss in one area of life affects other areas of life. What looks at first like a single loss is discovered to be a network of overlapping losses.[2] Some losses are material; others, physical or bodily. Most losses are experienced psychologically and spiritually as well.

Network Losses

The loss of a job, for example, can mean multiple losses at many levels of personal, family, and social life. Imagine that a person with primary responsibility for family income is given two weeks notice and has no prospects for a new job. You might reflect on how you would cope with such a situation.

The loss of the job is surely a *role* loss that is likely to result in identity confusion. It will also bring serious *material* loss as the family scrambles to pay bills. The breadwinner experiences herself as a failure, suffering the *psychological and spiritual* loss of self-confidence, a weakening of her sense of competence, and in extreme cases, the loss of faith and hope. She will suffer the loss of *relationships* within her career world as well as struggle and change within family and social relationships. Indeed, even *bodily* loss due to physical or psychological illness might follow in the wake of a career loss. The whole family system, itself a web of interconnections, as well as the well-being of each family member, shares in a *network* loss through the unwelcome changes in its life together.

Another illustration of a common network loss is the entry or leaving of a member from a group—from family or neighborhood or a social, public, or religious institution. When a person is no longer present, the whole system changes. A system must change also when someone new enters. Families undergo major systemic changes at births; at departures, when a child leaves for military life, college, or to live on his or her own; when children marry; and when family members die.

I remember a phone call from my sister the day her third and youngest daughter left for college. Struggling through unexpected tears, my sister grieved that family life would never be the same. I must remind her of that bleak Sunday afternoon almost twenty years ago, now that her daughter, with husband and three young children, has returned to my sister's home while their own house is being built. Network losses and gains are very much alive.

On a more serious level, consider the loss that results from betrayal or abuse. Not only is one's sense of value damaged, but when the offender is a trusted person, the positive image one had of him or her is shattered. Multiple losses follow such devastating experiences as child abuse or rape. A child loses her innocence, a right relationship with the abuser, a secure environment, her virginity—all damaging losses that will be felt for a long time, even a lifetime.

A rape victim suffers a complete loss of power through the loss of control of her body; she could not protect herself from violent invasion. She loses a sense of security, of normal stability. She may lose sleep and appetite and suffer headaches, stomach pains, and nausea. She loses her enjoyment of sexual experience. She undergoes a loss of confidence, as well as a loss of self-image. She might also feel the loss of faith, of hope, of happiness, of trust in humankind. There are network losses particularly felt by older adults. These can be roughly grouped as physical or bodily change and loss, including health; the loss of material possessions; and role loss. All of these losses are experienced psychologically and spiritually.

Network Losses in Aging

For many elders all over the world, becoming old means lack of employment, inadequate economic support, social isolation, serious material deprivation—poverty and even starvation.[3] In this country, although in general older people enjoy more material resources than in generations past, the millions of old people who live in poverty suffer increased material deprivation after sixty-five. They are not likely the readers of this book. This book will be read by people who live well above the poverty line, the sisters and brothers of those who live in destitution.

Physical Loss

Physical and bodily loss becomes a special focus for many older adults. Bodily changes in the later decades of life affect the way you perceive your appearance, your physical functioning, and often your health. What follows is a summary of common physical changes, several of them more problematic for women than for men.

Skin and tissue. Changes in elastin and collagen begin in the early to mid-forties, resulting in wrinkling of the skin, most notably the face, neck, and hands. Fatty tissue shifts from extremities to abdomen and hips, resulting in thinner arms and legs, sagging breasts, sunken eyes, and more visible bones.

Sensory. After forty, the lens and muscles of the eye lose elasticity, resulting in the need for magnification when reading. After fifty, one experiences a decrease in the ability to hear. After sixty, many persons have a weakened sense of smell and fewer taste buds.

Musculoskeletal. Muscle fibers decrease in size; bone mass undergoes a similar change after forty-five. Changes in the joints accelerate after forty; vertebra in the spine shorten. Women have particular trouble with loss of bone mass after menopause.

Heart and lung. The heart muscle becomes less efficient, resulting in a decreased output of blood. Elasticity of the lungs decreases.

Nervous system. Elders generally react to stimuli less rapidly and move more slowly, requiring more caution in movement.

Reproductive system. After thirty-five, women experience gradual, multiple changes in breasts, ovaries, uterus, cervix, and vagina. Menopause occurs at the average age of fifty.

Genitourinary. The bladder decreases in size and does not empty as completely.[4]

These bodily changes result in a diminishment of physical energy, a pervasive loss in old age. Many aging people experience the loss of energy as a loss of self-image: "I've always been able to do more." "I don't feel like my old self anymore." "This is not me."

Sensory changes often cause diminished hearing and sight. There is debate about how normal the loss of memory is in old age. Some believe that midlife memory concerns are basically the result of increased expectations of oneself and a failure to pay sufficient attention to what is going on in the environment.[5]

When my memory is occasionally sluggish I am reminded of the downside of age. A friend taught me a helpful way of retrieving details and avoiding frustration. The gimmick sometimes works. For example, I go downstairs and then can't remember why I've come to the basement. Standing in the middle of the floor, I say out loud, "My name is Carroll Saussy, and I came down here to . . . " The answer usually comes. Now and then I have to go back up to the spot where the impulse to descend originated to remember the treasure I wanted to retrieve. The loss of memory slows one down; it can also be disorienting.

While muscular and neurological losses are serious, perhaps the most common physical loss experienced among the older population, and particularly among women, is the loss of youthful appearance.

Aging women are not often regarded as physically attractive by the general population, but aging men are more often seen as appealing, even handsome. Both women and men resist the signs of age, acting as if aging were a disease rather than a gift for those who are fortunate enough to receive it. Bundles of money are spent by people of means to obscure the signs of old age.

Why do people hide their age? Concealing the signs of old age, or "passing" for someone younger, is deemed necessary because of the fear of rejection, denigration, and isolation that old people often experience among younger people. Another reason some may want to "pass" is because they do not feel as old as they know they look, and they want to look the way they feel. Finally, old people come to believe the cultural message that old is unattractive.

Old faces turn many people away. The external marks of age block a person from seeing inside to the heart and soul of life, where ultimate beauty lies. But one cannot listen to a saga about how an old person has met the challenges of life and come to peaceful self-acceptance without seeing beauty in the wrinkles that underscore the same story, etched line by line, across the storyteller's face.

Loss of Health

While physical change may be difficult to accept, one of the most dreaded bodily losses of old age is the loss of health, a loss that becomes increasingly threatening as one moves from young-old, to middle-old, to old-old. Pain and prolonged illness affect a person at all levels: physical, psychological, spiritual, and social. Many people learn to live with pain and illness with great courage and heroism; others are devastated by the experience. It is dangerous for people who enjoy good health and high energy to idealize aging. Old people who battle physical pain and overwhelming loss day in and day out have little energy left to think about satisfying or faithful aging. The strife between integrity and despair intensifies when physical illness limits a person's presence of mind and independence.

Reflective Pause

Recall a time when you felt miserably sick. Food was out of the question and your sleep was fitful. Perhaps days dragged by and you felt little or no improvement. You wondered how people around you could manage to get up and get going. You wondered if you would ever know energy and good health again. What adjectives describe you in that illness?

Did words like depressed, weak, or hopeless come up for you? Ill health can wipe out a sense of hope and purpose, even block the feeling of being loved. Relentless pain can deprive a person of a sense of well-being, energy, and possibility, and lead to despair.

A dreaded illness of our time is the loss of mental functioning at the onset of Alzheimer's disease, an illness that can devastate the whole family system. People understandably fear the possibility that not only their present relationships but also their histories could completely disappear from their consciousness. Family members know that they will lose the person they love long before death takes them. Although severe dementia resulting from Alzheimer's disease affects only 1 percent of persons sixty-five to seventy-four, it is suffered by 7 percent of persons from seventy-five to eighty-four, and 25 percent of those over eighty-five.[6]

Middle-aged women often experience an altered self-concept when they undergo a hysterectomy or mastectomy. Prostate surgery usually alters a man's physical functioning as well as his self-image. Patients who suffer an iatrogenic (doctor-induced) illness experience not only a health loss but a loss of faith in the medical profession. When people manage to live through physical agony, they look back and wonder how they survived. Many credit faith in God and the love of supportive family and friends for getting them through a bodily hell. In addition to good medical treatment, sometimes it is a sheer will to live that accounts for survivors' successful passage through extraordinary pain and critical illness.

Most of the serious illness, deterioration, and decline that old people suffer occurs in the last two years before their death. All adults experience periodic illness, deterioration, and decline, and certainly not every specific deterioration ought to be seen as a harbinger of the final days. Because it is usually only the last two years that are marked by serious deterioration and decline, however, why see the decades that constitute old age as determined by this aspect of human life? Such a link contributes to a harmful stereotype of old people as finished.

Material Loss

The loss of the automobile for those who can no longer drive safely and the loss of home for those who must move away from a place that has long been their nest are profound.

Securing a driver's license was surely a milestone for every adolescent and adult behind the wheel. Relinquishing that license because of diminished physical capacities feels more like a dreaded millstone than a promising milestone. (You might spend time reflecting on what it will be or was like to relinquish your car keys.)

The loss of home is a massive material loss for many older adults. Whether you move from a larger to a smaller residence, into the home of a child or sibling, or into a retirement or nursing home, the loss is dramatic. A well-known place with its familiar comforts and all that it meant to your sense of self is gone. The role you enjoyed as homeowner or renter of space that was in your control has also disappeared.

Your body suffers the change. The loss of context and neighborhood alters everyday relationships that shaped your life. For those moving into an institutional setting, the loss of privacy and of freedom or locus of control over the details of one's life can be shattering.

Notes written by a nursing home resident and found in her semiprivate room after her death were published in *Newsweek*. At eighty-four, confined to a wheelchair, Anna Mae Seaver described a typical day. She was awakened by the wheezing of the asthmatic woman in the next bed, a former chain smoker. After calling an aide who washed and helped her into her wheelchair, she was ready for a 67-minute wait for breakfast. She knew that some residents sat and waited . . . and wondered what they were waiting for. First breakfast. Only three hours and twenty-six minutes later comes lunch.

Lamenting the loss of privacy, Seaver closed the door to their room for time to herself when her roommate was in the TV room. Invariably an aide opened the door unannounced and walked in as if Seaver were not there, sometimes going into her drawers. Seaver wondered if she were invisible. Feeling that she had lost her right to respect and dignity, she pondered what might happen if the roles were reversed.

Seaver experienced the same lack of respect when staff persons used baby talk in addressing her. A certified teacher with a degree in music, she deplored having people position their faces directly in front of hers, and with raised voice address her with words like "deary." Once, after trying unsuccessfully to make her feelings known, she shouted at a staff person in frustration. She had asked for help more than a dozen times. At each request she received nothing more than condescending smiles and responses such as "All right, deary, I'm working on it." Something broke loose within her and Seaver uncharacteristically lost her temper. That time she wanted to be taken to a bathroom.[7]

It is important to note that only around 5 percent of old people live in institutions at any one time. Overall, elders have a 20 percent chance of spending some time in an institution before they die.[8] The myth that the self-centered American family has abandoned its elders is not true. Studies indicate that 85 percent of all elder care is provided by the family, as well as the bulk of emotional support of ill or disabled old people.[9] Nonetheless, many young old people fear the possible loss of their home and live with dreadful, stereotypical images of life in a nursing home.

Psychological and Spiritual Loss

Psychological and spiritual losses are undergone from within the self, such as the loss of self-image due to rejection, the loss of future possibilities after the onset of a progressively debilitating illness, the loss of relationships through death or illness, and the loss of faith in God or hope in humankind.

A sometimes subtle and often pervasive psychological and spiritual loss that accompanies aging is the denigration of old people conveyed through ageist attitudes. Old people lose the more positive images and expectations that were projected onto them at an earlier age. Especially within the work world, the next generation often cuts them out of the picture, leaving them isolated and alone. Ageism is encapsulated in stereotypical reactions to the elderly, the topic of the next chapter.

The loss of a treasured relationship is perhaps the deepest psychological and spiritual loss, short of debilitating physical or psychological illness. Relationships make life worth living. Solid relationships take time to develop; they have histories of their own. The shattering experience of the death of loved ones, especially partners and children, can tear a person's life apart, leaving an emptiness that the survivor takes to her or his own grave. Relational losses that result from deaths tend to accelerate in the last quarter of life. Many elders over eighty can recite litanies of those who have gone before them, but only a short list of surviving family and longtime friends.

Perhaps the most difficult death to cope with is the loss of a loved one through suicide. Guilt accompanies all deaths when one grieves over what one did or failed to do within relationship to the deceased. When faced with the suicide of a loved one, the guilt can be overwhelming. A full discussion of suicide is beyond the scope of this book. Suffice it to say that suicide among the elderly is a serious problem. People over sixty-five compromise 13 percent of this country's population and 19 percent of the suicides. Suicide among the elderly is the highest of any age group. Attempted suicides by elders are also more successful, with twice the rate than for other groups.[10]

Suicides most often follow depression; contrary to popular belief, late-life depression is not normal. Experts testifying before the U.S. Senate Special Committee on Aging were convinced that depression in the elderly can generally be reversed through professional treatment. Families and physicians must detect the signs of depression, such as accidental falls, sleeplessness, appetite and weight problems, refusing to take medication, heavy smoking, social withdrawal, lack of energy, loss of interest, not taking care of physical needs, and constipation—symptoms that go unnoticed because elders do not admit readily to feeling gloomy.[11] Helping depressed elders find something worth anticipating and worth doing can ward off suicide.

A common network loss in old age comes at retirement, a change of life with profound psychological and spiritual implications. Retirement from full-time work includes the loss of professional identity, role, and often much more. Retirement signals for many that the countdown has come; their days are numbered. Retirees frequently suffer identity confusion and feel dispensable, isolated, and alone. Studies of unemployed persons have indicated that work is so central to personal integrity that being removed from the regular work force is a potent factor in the disintegration of personality.[12] A retiree illustrates this conclusion:

> I ambled through the house from room to room, pacing the floor. I had recurring attacks of panic. The free time I had looked forward to enjoying was empty, and I made many false moves in an attempt to fill it . . . Believe me, it was one of the most distraught times of my entire life.[13]

The network losses suffered in retirement are amplified when people have over-identified with a job or career, thriving on the prestige or financial awards and benefits it afforded. Out on their own somewhere around age sixty-five, they no longer recognize themselves.

When people develop interests and hobbies outside "regular work," there need not be a dissolution of personality, though there might surely be the experience of loss. Unless people either acquire interests earlier in life or prepare for the later years by developing new horizons, they will be left bereft. Like aging, retirement sneaks up on those who do not anticipate the transition.

Social gerontologist Robert Atchley suggests four states in retirement. Retirement begins with a *retirement event*, which while experienced as bittersweet, is usually a high point for the retiree who is made tangibly aware of her or his significance to colleagues and friends. A *honeymoon period* generally follows, when the person is aware of new freedoms, the absence of work pressure, and as a colleague said upon his retirement, the opportunity to read the morning paper in the morning. The *third stage* is more difficult, a period marked by depression, disengagement, and sometimes despair. If the third stage can be worked through successfully, a *fourth stage* of new self-construction and meaning follows.[14]

People who prepare well for their retirement, with engaging projects underway and plans for the future in place, may be spared the third stage. Still employed full time, I speak out of hope rather than from experience. Faithful aging requires the anticipation and working through of whatever stages of retirement one confronts.

Some friends and neighbors have warned me that retirement is not all that it is cracked up to be; others say it is so much more. The difference might well be discovered in the diverse meanings that people project into their work. Six meanings have been suggested by researchers. Work is:

1. The basis for one's sense of worth.
2. An arena for making friends.
3. A source of prestige and recognition.
4. A source of new experiences, creativity, and self-expression.
5. An opportunity to serve others.
6. A way of passing time.[15]

When work is mostly a way to make money, retirement can be seen as attractive. The more meaning one found in work, the harder it will be to let the position go. Then, too, some people never retire. They work throughout old age, possibly reducing the hours of employment or moving from one work arena to another. Most people who live into their mid-seventies and eighties, however, do retire. No matter how meaningful one's career has been, people need to develop interests and hobbies, as well as relationships with persons of different ages, in order to be free to move into retirement with hopes, expectations, and adequate plans.

Conclusion

One of the major realities of age is that losses not only increase but become a dominant theme of elder life. Losses must be acknowledged and in some cases grieved. At the same time, an important sequel to dealing with loss is the recognition of gains that often follow. Loss challenges people to use their resources—sometimes ordinary coping skills, sometimes emergency survival skills. In either case, a person who works through a major loss learns something about herself or himself. What is learned can be experienced as a gain. Inevitably old age will hold an assortment of loss and suffering along with joy and fulfillment. A wise elder seeks depth of experience, depth of soul, even in the midst of loss. There is both loss and gain in the transformation.

Some losses that accompany aging must be reversed. For example, the loss of respect from younger people, often expressed through negative stereotypes, requires confrontation and the transformation of images. New representations of elders must be put in place. The next chapter takes on the challenge of stereotypes.

For Personal Reflection

1. Begin by brainstorming with yourself to draw up a list of major losses you have suffered. Look over your list and ask yourself if there is a specific loss with which you are now

struggling. Is this a loss that you have not adequately grieved? What might you need to do or say to bring closure to the
loss?

2. Are you aware of needs that your losses have left unful-
filled? Are there ways in which these needs might be met?

3. What roles would you never let go? In what ways do
these roles define you?

4. Look back over your list of losses and note any gains
that you have experienced through the way you responded
to the loss. What have you learned through the losses you
have survived?

5. Are there losses that you joyfully celebrate? What gain
have you enjoyed through gladly giving something up?

Meditation

When I look at your heavens, the work of your fingers,
the moon and the stars that you have established;
what are human beings that you are mindful of them,
mortals that you care for them? (Psalm 8: 3-4)

Imagine a setting that is rich with many of the good
things you most enjoy. Picture the place, the people, the
things that surround you in that setting. Perhaps this environment will remind you of other blessings that have graced
your life. If your imagination takes you to yet other places,
go with it, aware of the many delights that have been a part
of your life. Your task is to bask in happy experiences—from
childhood, from adolescence, in adult life. If negative
thoughts enter your consciousness, try to gently put them
aside and stay with what is good and true and beautiful. . . .
Spend whatever time you need relishing these gifts. . . . Who
are you that God is mindful of you?

When I look at your heavens, the work of your fingers,
the moon and the stars that you have established;
what are human beings that you are mindful of them,
mortals that you care for them?

Now project yourself into the future. You are an old person, and many of the good experiences you remembered a few minutes ago are clearly a part of your past. What do you have to let go? How do you deal with the loss? What will replace these valuable experiences? Spend time in the presence of the Holy One, in conversation if that works for you, in silence if you choose. Be aware that you are not alone and that nothing from your past is gone forever. . . . Who are you that God is mindful of you? . . . Conclude your meditation with the words:

When I look at your heavens, the work of your fingers,
the moon and the stars that you have established;
what are human beings that you are mindful of them,
mortals that you care for them?

Further Reflection

The questions and meditation may have revealed to you how you most want to live and what you can and cannot live without. It might be helpful to gather symbols of the things and people and roles that are most important to you and keep them visible as you continue to work through this book. In what ways do these things give you back to yourself?

3

Refusing the Stereotypes, Discovering New Images

It is assumed by very well-meaning and dedicated people that somehow in the upper age brackets we enter a second childhood when we become not mature, responsible elders of the tribe but wrinkled babies. Much of what is done for us and to us, instead of with us, hastens the onslaught of wrinkled babyhood.

—*Maggie Kuhn,*
"Spiritual Well-Being as a Celebration of Wholeness"

THE LOSSES FACED BY ELDERS ARE exacerbated by the social attitudes that add to the struggle of aging. While aging people ought not accept negative images projected onto them, they might best begin their campaign to replace those images by accepting the fact that the strong denial of aging and death by young and middle adults will, in fact, be a reality. Likewise, one can expect but need not accept the social isolation proffered them as they grow old. Down with the notion of wrinkled babyhood!

This chapter considers how young people and not-as-old-adults view the old. Stereotypes, many negative but some promising, emerge from such attitudes. In addition to reviewing stereotypes that are projected onto elders, we will explore alternative images of old age. Two illustrations conclude the chapter. A personal experience with the Women Health's Initiative is used to illustrate shifting images of aging women. Finally, a recent book that grew out of a discussion among older women about their perceptions of their own aging is reviewed.

Attitudes Toward Old Age

Generalizations are dangerous, but patterns do emerge in the way the old are perceived and portrayed. Children who have been in relationship with caring older people generally accept old people for who and what they are: different from children, often kind, usually wrinkled and gray folks who notice them and are happy to be in the presence of children. Interest is often mutual and conversation straightforward. Children who have not had contact with old people, or have experienced only cranky old people, are afraid of them.

The American Association of Retired Persons conducted a study of 400 children between six and eleven. The children were asked to draw an old person and a young person in the same picture, and then were invited to talk about their drawings and about aging. The older children drew more negative pictures and expressed more negative feelings about aging than the younger ones. Children drawing an old person whom they knew drew kindlier faces than those who drew a generalized old person.[1]

The diverting of eyes away from elders and loss of interest in them generally comes after childhood. Youth have their own interests, and old people do not often figure in them. Listen to a conversation among a group of young people about elders.

"There are so many old people now. Everybody is staying alive too long. It sounds cruel, especially when you think of your own relatives, but I think that after about the age of seventy there should be euthanasia. It is a shame that so many old people are kept alive. They waste the tax-payer's money and fill up the geriatric wards and everything."

"Linda," says Pat, "you don't really believe that?"

"Yes," says Linda, "I do. I do, I do, I do!"

"At seventy? One of my aunties is seventy and she's just incredible. The way she goes on she could be about twenty. Lots of relations on my father's side have been pensioned-off but they're certainly no burden at all."

"My gran is seventy-five and she still goes dancing twice a week," says Colin. "She's gone dancing twice a week since the war. She's one of those nineteen-forties ladies, you know."

"Dancing when you're old," says Linda, "how could she? . . . "

"The old are jokes," says Pat. "Colin has proved it."[2]

When she was a student in gerontology at age twenty-five, Patricia Moore set out to discover firsthand the social attitudes toward old people. She transformed herself into an eighty-year-old. Wearing splints on her knees that altered her walking, clouded contact lenses that impaired her vision, and folds of latex that wrinkled her face, she took to the streets of New York. She was ignored or cursed for being clumsy; she was shortchanged by merchants; she was mugged by a gang of boys; her purse was stolen. Moore believes that attitudes toward elders have improved since her experience in 1979, but that ageism, which is learned behavior, continues because people are taught to denigrate old people. Her recommendation: children should be shown love at the hands of older people. She clings to the hope that the attitudes toward elders will change.[3]

Ideas about old people held by both children and youth are shaped by the frequency and quality of their exposure to old people. The real isolation of many old people in this country is caused by young and middle-aged adults, those who make decisions regarding living arrangements that dramatically affect the lives of elders. The old-old who are able to live in their own homes or within multigenerational communities seem to live more satisfying lives than old people warehoused together.

The old are seen as a geometrically multiplying mass of major health-care consumers threatening the economic stability of the country. Looking ahead, demographers provide unwelcome projections about the huge wave of baby boomers on the gray horizon, highlighting problems heightened by increased longevity and the astronomical costs of medical care. The shifting of population curves in this country is clearly a significant concern that requires change and careful planning at many levels of society. Without doubt, the spiraling increase of medical costs and the numbers of old people without adequate medical care is alarming. Increased longevity, however, is also a symbol of technological success and a cause for celebration. Although society is preoccupied with the fact that more people are reaching old age, it fails to recognize the wonderful scientific advance this new fate signals. Instead of celebrating the fact that by the year 2000 many people in the U.S. will be assured a full life, people anxiously cry that by the year 2000 half of the population will be over sixty.[4]

"There are too many of them," "they have too much political power," and "they cost too much," are the dominant messages that pervade public conversations about elders. What do people do when they have too much of anything? Give it away? Put it out with the trash? Have a yard sale? Or maybe put it in an attic or garage where it is out of sight.

The old-old are all too often warehoused off by themselves. The young-old and middle-old are given titles such as "senior citizens" or "golden-agers" and offered reduced admission fees. These are experienced, mature adults, many of whom feel a serious responsibility for their communities. Others simply live, without motivation, without encouragement, wasting their years in trivial pursuits.

Perhaps elders received greater respect when there were not too many of them, yet negative images of aging are as old as the Hebrew Bible. One can expect gray hair (1 Samuel 12:2), loss of eyesight (Genesis 27:1), loss of hearing (2 Samuel 19:35), loss of potency—either of enjoyment (Genesis 18:12) or ability to impregnate or to conceive (Genesis 18:11, 2 Kings 4:14).

Today there are remedies for poor eyesight, and poor hearing, and quick fixes for those who choose not to honor their gray hair. While elders know that sexual enjoyment is available to them, the younger generations are not often ready to recognize the sexual wants, needs, and satisfying experiences of the old.

Studies indicate that old people's self-perceptions are far more positive than the perceptions projected onto them by youth and middle age. For example, persons under fifty-five believe that older people are lonely; a majority of older people claim that they are seldom lonely.[5] While elders may be perceived as rigid, narrow-minded, ineffective, and finished, their own experience of old age is often quite the opposite. Jungian analyst Florida Scott-Maxwell acknowledged that her age puzzled her. She anticipated a quiet time, thought her seventies were interesting and relatively serene. Her eighties, by contrast, were filled with passion and intensity.

Far from being rigid or finished, she was bursting with life, profoundly enjoying the discovery of herself.[6]

Perhaps the major damage that results from distorted social attitudes toward old age is *isolation*, surely one of the most painful and unnecessary aspects of growing old. To isolate any group of people is to make them invisible to the rest of the community. When the old are warehoused in retirement homes or when elders choose senior settlements with only their kind, the world inside and outside such environments suffers the loss of intergenerational living. The processes of aging are secluded from general society, and everyone is deprived. The old are seen as different, even shameful. Not only are they hidden, but those from whom they are hidden are deprived of seeing their own future and knowing that it can be rich and rewarding.

Maggie Kuhn had such strong resistance to the typical church-sponsored segregated housing that she wanted to see every such development then underway stopped and the plans destroyed. The new plans should include child-care centers, nursery schools, and tutoring arrangements with the very young. This might correct the oppression created by the idea that elders want to live by themselves. Kuhn also resisted the belief that every lonely widow should be allowed to live alone in her big old home. What that elder needs and what all need, Kuhn believed, is a communal-cooperative lifestyle, with shared space and shared human resources.[7]

The isolation of elders creates a Catch-22. Attitudes can hardly change unless the old are in the midst of people of all ages. Together, old and young, all of whom age, could come to a profound acceptance of the human condition. Conscious of a common destiny, the young would not choose to isolate the old and the old would not need to dread aging. Only then will the more promising realities of old age flourish.

Some Negative Stereotypes of Old People

Stereotypes are pernicious. Those who do the stereotyping end up seeing what they expect to see. Those most hurt by stereotypes are weak people who fulfill the stereotypes, adapting to the characteristics projected onto them.

Reflective Pause

Before I suggest some of the prevailing stereotypes of old people, I ask you to get in touch with your own. What conventional ideas about aging have you absorbed? What has lived experience taught you?

As a warm-up, write the word age *or* old age *at the center of a piece of paper and circle it. Using a technique that Gabriele Rico calls "clustering," let whatever bubbles up in your imagination spill out all over the page. The purpose here is to let your creative right brain have its say before your rational, logical left brain takes over. Words pouring out might follow one another in groups that hold together. Then perhaps a new cluster of related words will pop into your imagination and onto the page. Follow the new image until still another notion enters your imagination, circling words and using lines and arrows to connect circles that tend to cluster. No censoring. Just write. In the midst of the spill, you may experience an "Aha" moment that shifts your mental activity from uncensored clustering to the urge to express yourself in a sentence or in verse. Rico calls this the "trial web shift." The shift is from a broad web of words, to the intentional focus on a particular image or insight. Go with the "aha" and write.*

Spending over a year immersed in literature on aging, my attitudes about growing old are in the midst of a rewarding creative transformation. Following my own advice, I clustered *age* and was encouraged by the words that spilled out on my page: *freedom, generativity, possibility, desire, urgency, hope, relationship.*

For the sake of unearthing stereotypes, I decided to cluster the down side of aging, and was surprised when I wrote *dead age* at the middle of the page and circled it. I wove a stereotypical web, using such words as *finished, bored, smelly, withered, useless, blank, passive,* and *drab.* The words *spare me* triggered what Rico calls the "trial web shift." *Spare me* stopped me in my tracks. I moved from random thoughts and fragmented images to a sentence with a very concrete image. "Spare me the fate of the wheelchair wall." (I hope my image does not offend persons with disabilities who need to use a wheelchair. The wheelchair wall, built by lining up old people in wheelchairs, is for the convenience of their institutional caregivers.)

The image surfaced from several sources. One is a description by nursing home resident Anna Mae Seaver. She lamented her diminished life in a wheelchair, asking her readers if they ever sat in a wheelchair over an extended period of time. Wheelchairs are not comfortable. Their occupants are squeezed in the middle, with constant pressure applied to the hips; the armrests are often too narrow. Seaver believed herself luckier than those who are strapped into wheelchairs and abandoned, captive prisoners, in front of the television.[8]

In a nursing home I have visited on numerous occasions, some of the frailest residents are wheeled into a row across from the nurses' station and near the elevator. Stepping off of the elevator has always been a difficult moment for me.

The sights and sounds and smells that confront me are depressing. Once I asked the woman I visited about the row of chairs, especially about a resident who often wailed as she waited and watched. I wondered what effect the continual wailing had on the other residents. My friend said she no longer heard the cries of this chronic complainer.

One day I stepped off the elevator to see for the first time in the lineup the woman I visited. More alert than the rest along the wall, still she seemed dispirited to have joined the sentries. My friend didn't live much longer. Here's what I wrote when I clustered "dead age," an expression I had never used before.

> Spare me the fate of the
>   wheelchair wall.
> A role reversal,
>   these bent sentries being watched
>   by guarded eyes at the nursing station.
> Waiting and watching—
>   now mute, now mumble, now moan.
> The hands on the large clock march tediously
>   toward the next bland meal.
> Drab and pale,
>   in faded pink and blue and gray,
>   they keep watch.
> Slumped,
>   dragged down,
>   stooped forward,
>   looking nowhere.
> Seeing there and then, and here and now,
>   sadness and grief and loneliness—
>   has-beens
>   calling out for notice.

> How long a day,
>   how long a life,
>   a long banal bore in the nursing home.
> Spare me.
> Spare me the fate of the
>   wheelchair wall.

Reality or stereotype? Perhaps a mingling of both. Surely this is what I have seen in some nursing homes, over and over. In 1975, psychiatrist and aging advocate Robert Butler commented on his survey of commercial nursing homes. His conclusion was that nursing homes are facilities with few or no nurses and hardly qualify as homes.[9]

Only a small minority of elders in this country, most of them old-old, live in nursing homes. Many nursing-home residents are content and feel blessed to be cared for by kind hands and hearts. There are nursing homes and nursing homes, but I doubt that many readers look forward to even the best available.

Prophets for the elderly would avoid nursing homes for most who occupy them. Eighteen outstanding advocates for the aged are honored in the book *Profiles in Caring*, including Congressman Claude Pepper, physician Elisabeth Kübler-Ross, Senator Frank Moss, and activist Maggie Kuhn.[10] The eighteen unanimously support affordable home health care, a service that would allow many elders to remain in their homes.

For some, nursing homes are a necessity, and unfortunately, the stereotype of the nursing home comes much too close to the reality. The next chapter includes one of the exceptions; there are many more. Nonetheless, the stereotype I carry of *old-old* is of isolated persons, bored from dawn to dark, watching and waiting for meals, for visitors, for death—finished. It is a dreadful stereotype.

The Old as Finished

Congressman Pepper helped shatter the stereotype of the old as senile, decrepit and powerless. He knew and proved through his own life that people can grow, learn, and live productive lives into their nineties and beyond. In 1977 Pepper became chair of the House Select Committee on Aging. He brought six centenarians as witnesses before the committee, lively people who were continuing to make meaningful contributions to their country. None was senile, decrepit, or powerless.

The stereotype persists of the old as finished, without enough energy to do much more than vegetate. While there were certainly negative images of old age before Otto von Bismarck, the German social reformer, his success in removing persons over sixty from the active work force contributed to the old being seen as decrepit and unfit for work. Bismarck founded disability and unemployment insurance in the 1880s in order to move sixty-year-olds out of the work force and make room for unemployed younger people. While U.S. law now prohibits mandatory retirement, many employers find ways of pushing people out of their ranks simply because they are sixty-five. The stereotype of sixty-five as retirement age works.

Many middle-aged people, buying into the stereotype and projecting perhaps their own loss of vitality, believe that those over sixty-five lack energy—that they are tired and listless and ready to stop working. Elders know that they can do more than society encourages them to do.

The Old as Physically Unattractive

Who says that there is something intrinsically unattractive, even repulsive, about aging skin and bones? Too many people in this country become old believing that young is beautiful and old is ugly. For the land of the free, read *young;* and the home of the brave, read *attractive.*[11] This is the land noted for a radical increase in cosmetic surgery such as face-lifts and nose jobs in the 1960s, when old age and old bodies were seriously devalued by baby boomers.[12]

Gail Sheehy calls the loss of youthful looks the *vanity crisis,* prevalent in both women and men as they move into second adulthood and toward the "flaming fifties." There were few surprises in Sheehy's recounting of the agonies women experience when they perceive that they have "lost their looks." The surprises came as Sheehy described a men's group in which individuals shared their intense struggle around losing hair. A fifty-nine year old wailed that he hated his hair. He pulled it down, curled it over, despaired that there was nothing he could do to cover this indelible mark of age. This man's sense of loss was echoed by others in the group.

On the one hand, appearance is important. Taking care of one's body and its grooming does matter and is a reflection of how a person feels about herself or himself. On the other hand, rejecting the appearance of elders because they look their age is hurtful to both the beholder and the beheld and an insult to God's creation. For the old person to find her or his own appearance unacceptable clearly leads to self-rejection and low self-esteem.

One wonders, what is so repulsive about old bodies that clearly look their appropriate age? Wrinkled skin; thin, graying hair or bald heads; folds of loose skin under the neck; flabby flesh on arms and legs; bent bones; deformed hands and feet; abundant waistlines—why are these features deemed intrinsically ugly? What would it take for younger people to see something different when they look at the body of an old person? And what would it take for old people to see something different when they look in the mirror—to accept what they see as distinguished? Weathered faces, lined by years of lived experience; a smile of contentment, perhaps of appreciation for interest shown and respect received from others; seasoned bodies with well used limbs and bones, well worked hands and feet—all belong to human beings with tales to tell.

Psychiatrist Robert Coles's interviews with elders of Spanish and Pueblo Indian descent are recorded in *The Old Ones of New Mexico,* complete with exquisite photographs of strong women and men with weathered faces and piercing eyes. A woman in her nineties says that a ten-year-old asked what it will be like for her to turn one hundred. She put her hand beside the boy's and they compared skin. The old woman explained that "it is good to be young and it is good to be old." She said the boy needed no further explanation.

Wise children know that people are far more than their looks, far more than their bodies. A six-year-old said that her bedridden grandmother's body was getting smaller. Grandma was not shrinking, she added, only her body.[13]

The Old as Burdens

In reviewing negative attitudes toward the aging, we introduced the stereotype of the old as a burden, an immense financial burden society bears (and avoids) in caring for their medical needs. In addition to the monetary costs of elder care, there are weighty physical and emotional costs in providing for frail elders.

When people are unable to attend to their basic needs, others must help them. Babies cannot care for themselves. Children require ongoing care. The sick need various levels of assistance, no matter their age. Frequently the very old need help in taking care of their physical needs.

All people who depend on others for physical and emotional help can be experienced as burdens. Life *is* burdensome. Jobs and careers are burdensome. Women are burdened with an unfair amount of physical care of both young and old. The average woman spends around thirty years of her life caring first for children, later for aged parents. It is quite possible that a woman in her fifties working outside the home has an adolescent or young adult child at home, and both a mother and grandmother in need of ongoing care. She might have grandchildren pulling at her heartstrings as well.

The social challenge is twofold: 1) to find ways that people who are experienced as burdens can give as well as receive and can experience themselves as givers; and 2) to find ways for caregivers to share the burden of caring for parents, spouses, siblings, or children with others within their families, neighborhoods, and social networks. Not easily done.

Some old people are not a financial burden on society. Both median income and poverty rates vary greatly among subgroups of persons over sixty-five. Sex, race, ethnicity, and marital status affect the income and lifestyle of the old as well. Since the 1960s, the poverty rate among elders in this country has been reduced from roughly a third to an eighth. Some old people are burdens. Some are not. Twelve percent represents far too many old persons, however, who continue to live suffering lives below the poverty level.

Old Women as Discards

While both women and men struggle against stereotypes of aging, women have the harder task. There are mythical prototypes of women such as the cantankerous old witch, the frustrated old maid, the tottering bag lady, the overpowering bad mother, the arthritic bag of bones, and the little old lady. How does an old woman come into her own identity walking through such a mine field?

Aging women face at least double jeopardy, sometimes triple or quadruple. Aging women are denigrated because of age and sex; women of color and poor women are further disvalued. (One might think that lesbian elders would experience an additional jeopardy. Older lesbians, however, report an easier aging experience than heterosexual women. A possible explanation is that they have lived for years with the label "deviant" and can better deal with the additional social stigma that comes with old age.)

The bottom line is that the face of aging is largely a female face. Not only are there more of them, old women are poorer than old men. The poverty rate increases at each stage of old age; it is significantly higher for elderly women (16 percent) than elderly men (9 percent). The rate is higher still for elderly African Americans (33 percent) and Hispanics (22 percent) than for whites (11 percent). Elderly women are more likely to live alone. Most elderly men are married; most elderly women are not.[14]

In, "Growing Old Is Largely a Job for Women," Abigail Trafford takes her reader to the Washington Home, a Medicaid-funded nursing home in the District of Columbia. Most of the patients are women over eighty. With one hundred and eighty beds, the Washington Home is staffed by women physicians, has a nine-bed hospice unit headed by a woman, women nurse practitioners and social workers. Most of the nurses and nursing assistants are women. The support group for family caregivers is made up of all women. Where are the men? The executive director and financial officer of the facility are male. In this case, growing old is largely a job for women under male leadership.

Old women are considered discards because they have lost the roles that society has assigned to them. When women are no longer sex objects, no longer fruitful wombs, no longer caretakers of the very young or the very old, no longer wage earners, who are they? They are discards. Besides, there are too many of them, and they often lack financial, social, or political power. To overcome societal rejection, old women need to continue their work for justice. They also need friendship, respect, and challenge. If they do not discard one another, the stereotype of their "discardability" will lose its power and make way for an image of bonded, growing old women.

Positive Images of Aging

In honoring eighteen famous elders, attorney-at-law Val Halamandaris called them treasures, more valuable to the country than "all the gold in Fort Knox." How often are elders so valued?

The innumerable gifts of age include the fruits of the Spirit: "love, joy, peace, patience, kindness, generosity, faithfulness, gentleness and self-control" (Ephesians 5:22). All of these gifts can flourish in old age.

Reflective Pause

Think for a moment about an old person you have known personally or through the media who has been particularly inspiring to you. What adjectives would you use to describe this person?

My guess is that the words you chose included the notion of care, concern, kindness, and unselfishness. Erik Erikson's term *generativity* includes all of these virtues. Generativity is lively *care* for present and future generations, the generosity of adulthood that marks the life of faithful elders. Wise elders are eager to see others thrive. Grateful for their own success in facing the demands and struggles of their lives, grateful to be alive, generative elders have a sense of purpose that includes service to others. Generativity includes passion and commitment; its opposite is self-absorption.

Generative elders are able to move beyond selfish wants and needs to genuinely care for the generations. They actively seek opportunities to give themselves in service and support to others. Especially when they are gifted with good health and economic resources, they are in a prime position to embody the virtue of generativity. They rejoice with those who rejoice and weep with those who weep. Generative interests transcend self-interests; generative pursuits transcend a single lifetime. Generativity dreams dreams for tomorrow's world and helps build them today.

Some elders will express their generativity in a less public and grand a way than elder Eugene M. Lang. Nonetheless, his story beautifully illustrates generativity, writ large. In 1981 Lang promised the sixty-one students in the sixth-grade graduating class at an East Harlem public school to send them to college if they graduated from high school. More than half went to college. He stayed in touch with them all, continuing to encourage those who failed and helping them find jobs.

Five years later Lang founded the "I Have a Dream" foundation. By 1993 the Foundation had 145 projects, making scholarships available to over ten thousand students in forty-three cities. Patrons pledge $300,000 for a class and guarantee $2,000 to each student during each year of college.[15]

There are similar illustrations of scores of individuals who make generative decisions to offer their financial resources and personal efforts to improve the lives of people who do not have access to the same advantages. Collections of such stories would make for uplifting, encouraging reading.

Searching for a Title

Some people over sixty-five like being called "senior citizens" or "golden agers." Others might favor actress Helen Hayes's word "maturians," or Catherine Pacheco's titles for those who thoroughly resist the notion of withdrawal and inactivity after retirement, "pattern breakers" and "recommencers." I prefer Maggie Kuhn's choice, "the elders." For many women, the rediscovered "crone" is also full of possibility.

Elders are brave, wise, resilient, generative, and spirited persons who live from the depths of their souls and are open to change. Elders feel responsible for the common good. In many churches elders are awarded special roles within the congregation. Elders respect others and in turn are treated with respect.

Before the birth of Christianity, the crone was the tribal matriarch. Women are reappropriating the image of the crone, the wise woman celebrated by both youth and age who ministers to all ages. The crone is spiritual guide and healer. Many women discard Webster's definition of crone as "a withered old woman."

Croning rituals recognize and bless the life of older women. Some women ask to be croned at fifty; others wait until sixty or seventy. The croning takes place within a group of sisters, sometimes brothers as well. Crone Carol Scinto, seventy, delighted in her glorious croning, shared with four grown daughters, her husband, two grandchildren, and "baby brother" of fifty-seven. She said, "The result is one septuagenarian ready to climb another mountain, singing and dancing inside my wrinkles." Indeed, the crone can provide a promising image of old age to which many might aspire.

The Old as Wise

Among the more positive stereotypes of old age is that elders are *wise*. Wise people have a solid sense of self. Wise people not only know themselves well, they know what human life is all about and what makes people tick, and they know that every life is filled with ambiguity. Undaunted by paradox, change, and contradiction, wise people discover their direction in the midst of ambivalence. They know the difference between substance and trivia. They know what is important and they know how to compromise. Lived experience has brought them a seasoned sense of what's worth knowing and doing and worrying about. The wisdom of age is to be lifted up, embraced, and plumbed for the wealth of knowledge and insight acquired over many years of day-to-day existence in an ambiguous, unjust world.

The Old as Free

Poet and novelist May Sarton calls her emancipation the freedom to be absurd, to forget because the world around you expects you to forget, and the freedom to be eccentric coupled with freedom to be quite set in one's ways.[16] Social activist Maggie Kuhn expressed her freedom when she vowed on her eightieth birthday to do something outrageous at least once a week. She didn't let anything interfere with her commitment.[17]

If freedom is a gift of age, and if nonconformity and eccentricity are fueled by freedom, one might anticipate increased nonconformity in a population of elders. Eccentrics free themselves from many social restraints and in the process have better health and enjoy greater contentment.[18]

At eighty-five, Nadine Stair speculated on what she might do differently if she had another life to live. Surely she would take more risks and make more mistakes; she would limber up and be more relaxed. Although in her first life she was serious, sensible, and sane, in a second life she would be sillier. She would take more excursions, climb more mountains, swim more rivers, eat more ice cream but fewer green beans. While she might know more actual troubles, she would have fewer imaginary ones. On her return trip she would live in the present moment—lots of present moments. Confessing that she is the type who travels with thermometer, hot water bottle, raincoat, and parachute, she declared that the next time round she would travel light. You would find her in bare feet early in the spring and late into the fall. She would go to more dances, ride more merry-go-rounds, and pick more daisies.[19]

In other words, Nadine Stair would claim her freedom earlier in life. (I have taken her advice, and kick my shoes off earlier in the spring, enjoy bare feet deeper into the fall.) A person who claims freedom can be open and honest. A free person can be herself and describe life as she perceives it, without phoniness or pretense or ulterior motive. He can voice his wisdom. A free person can take risks, practice fresh behaviors, explore novel pastimes, and develop new hobbies. He can use his time and talent to nurture old relationships and develop new ones. Free people no longer are controlled by the demands of a false self in search of distorted ego needs—to be super responsible, to be liked by everyone, to succeed in all pursuits. Free people can be good to themselves. They indulge in personal enjoyment. They take great delight in comforts such as food and drink, bed and bath.

They delight too in art and music and drama. They know how to enjoy themselves in times of abundance and to hang on when life seems grim. Free people can't be bought. In full possession of themselves, they are not possessed by their possessions.

This is a significant aspect of freedom: freedom from possession by one's possessions. I say this as a person who takes great joy in beautiful things—not expensive collectors' items, but a simply and artfully decorated home. It expands my soul to sit in favorite spots in my modest home and ponder the fact that I thoroughly enjoy its beauty and also know that I could and will give it up. In the meantime, I relish my surroundings, find God in the place I call home, and resist being possessed by these simple possessions. Some years from now my concern will turn to distributing what I have collected, perhaps even finding God in a much smaller space. Material life will be reduced. Freedom is available in it all.

Soon after her one hundredth birthday, I asked Antoinette Gill to share with me some of her wisdom. A widow and retired auditor for the Internal Revenue Service, Antoinette moved into a retirement village after she broke her hip in her mid-nineties. Her response to my query about what she had learned through her years was brief and simple: "Don't worry." In other words, free yourself from worry. I waited for more words, but she stopped there. How many hours of the day are wasted in worry?

There is another aspect of freedom that comes with age. The intellectual and spiritual needs of elders change. Elders don't need all the answers to their philosophical and theological questions. Creed matters less; religious values matter more. With little concern about the dogmatic claims that divide denominations or faith groups, elders are able to embrace others with greater sincerity.[20]

The Old as Vitally Engaged in Life

Vital engagement means different things to different people. For those who have labored long and hard and received inadequate compensation, vital engagement in old age may well translate into leisurely reading and genuine recreation and relaxation. Vital engagement may mean a comfortable chair and a good book. Physically spent elders need to give the body a rest and the spirit a lift. Others feel compelled to engage in organized or individual activity that will make a difference to people in need. Still others require motivation to find satisfying engagement of any kind.

Congressman Claude Pepper toured the country in his eighties to stimulate interest in health insurance and home-care coverage for the aging. In a speech he proclaimed that the senior citizens of America, 28 million strong, "have left their rocking chairs and taken up placards."[21] Under the leadership of people like Claude Pepper and Maggie Kuhn, elders became aging activists, sending wake up calls to their colleagues to join their ranks. Some have poured their energies into seeking justice for elders through politics. Others have continued the work of elders of previous generations, volunteering their time in social and charitable endeavors. Kuhn left a "laundry list" for those seeking vital engagement in their elder years.

1. Test new lifestyles, such as cooperative, communal living.
2. Build new coalitions among young and old, black and white, rich and poor.
3. Become watchdogs of public bodies: observing the courts, watching city councils, monitoring the public bodies where critical decisions are made.
4. Advocate for consumers' rights, blowing the whistle on fraud, corruption, and poor services for elders.

5. Monitor corporate power and responsibility through watching media, protesting in stockholders' meetings for the sake of workers' safety and a protected environment.

6. Become healers of a sick society.

7. Become critical analysts of contemporary society and planners for its future directions.[22]

The Old as Learners

Elders have returned to the classroom and entered the studio, the computer lab, their own workshops. Whether taking a course at an educational institution or developing a new skill or hobby on their own, elders are taking new risks and reaping rewards.

For example, Jacob, a school administrator in New York, retired at fifty-nine. He needed a new challenge. His next step was teaching education courses. Jacob's road was blocked by a heart attack and an unexpected detour; he underwent open-heart surgery and a quadruple bypass before he resumed his next career. At sixty-seven, he entered law school and was subsequently hired by a law firm to work with seniors.[23] A gift to his aging peers! Colleges across the country are enriched by inspiring elders who return to the classroom and reinvent their lives; citizens at large are blessed by the wise contributions to the common good of many senior graduates.

Artist and Health Pioneer

Two additional new images of age lure me into a vital future. One is the artist. She is wonderfully herself, some would say eccentric. She rises early and anticipates inspiration. I see her standing, arms stretched above her head as she welcomes the rising sun. She is wedded to no specified art form because she is the artist in every woman and every man. She is an expression of God's creativity herself. My artist does not deny mortality; its awareness is itself inspiration.

My second image of a faithful elder is the health pioneer. She became a vital part of my life as I woke up to new possibilities and entered into faithful aging. In December 1995 I made one of the best decisions of my life. I called the Women's Health Initiative and volunteered to join their investigation of older women's health. With few studies in the past focused on health concerns of women, the National Institutes of Health has sponsored a decade-long research project involving more than 160,000 women between fifty and seventy-nine in fourteen cities in the nation.

I felt uncertain, vulnerable, curious, and full of anticipation when I emerged from the underground Eastern Market Metro station in Washington, D.C., to walk into the offices of the Women's Health Initiative for the first time. I knew that I was entering an unfamiliar place as a learner, that I had made a commitment of time and energy—and I fully anticipated the emergence of something new in my life. It was an intense moment, the beginning of great learning experience.

The preliminary paperwork landed me in a "diet change" group. Before the screening, I would have said that mine was a healthy diet—three meals a day, enough fruits and vegetables, vitamin supplements, not much red meat. For years I have exercised with some regularity. Probably because of olive oil, cheese, nuts, and more red meat in my diet than recommended, the computer listed me among people who needed some new eating habits.

My education about fat grams began when the dietitian held up unappetizing plastic models of food items, detailing the number of fat grams in each piece. The pat of butter did it. Four grams in a teaspoon, twelve in a tablespoon, and my daily goal was 24 grams of fat! Since that moment of truth, I have changed my diet dramatically, tried many recipes from Dean Ornish's *Eat More, Weigh Less*, lost ten pounds, exercised three to five times a week, gained greater appreciation for my body—and I have eliminated butter and margarine almost completely. I feel energetic, alert, vigorous, and younger. As much as I despise the "you're not getting older, you're getting better" philosophy, I heard myself mouthing those ridiculous words on a bike ride recently when my husband commented on how much more vigorously I pedaled on the uphill section of the path than I had when we last used the route. I know I have been very good to my body, and I feel abundantly blessed. A major life change at sixty-one.

I am the only European-American in a group of thirteen women. The other women are African American; I am blessed to have been welcomed into their circle. Our age range is fifty to seventy-six. The facilitated group met once a week for six weeks, every other week for six weeks, and now once a month for nine months. After that we will meet on our own. A core of approximately seven of us are regularly and enthusiastically present. Since the cutback to monthly meetings, we call one another with encouragement between sessions. In truth, I do not need much encouragement; my commitment feels irreversible. I thoroughly enjoy staying in touch with the women, however. To my surprise, I can't bring myself to eat some of the fat foods I enjoyed so much before my conversion, and easily turn down desserts that were once delights. I have gained a great appreciation for the tastes and textures of natural foods: grains and herbs of all kinds, vegetables without added oil, breads that stand alone. My new body simply won't consider more than an occasional taste of high fat foods.

There are really three gifts here: a new body, a new group of spirited, humorous risk takers, and my husband's interest in everything I've learned and his satisfaction with the new cuisine. He does most of the grocery shopping and regularly brings home "fat-free" treasures. He has also lost weight and joined me in regular exercise.

As I discover that some clothes hang loose, I remember a conversation with a friend in which she confessed that she willingly got rid of clothes that no longer fit. "At our age," she protested, "you deserve the right to spread out and you don't have to worry much about diet or weight. Buy new clothes." She and I, in our fifties at the time, are a month apart in age. I took note of her message, thinking maybe I was too vigilant about diet. Today, I know she is wrong. Aging women very much need to concern themselves with fat in their diets; there's no good reason to spread out. While the primary goal of the Women's Health Initiative is to understand how diet, hormone-replacement therapy, calcium, and vitamin D might prevent heart disease, cancer, and bone fractures, the gains it offers its participants exceed those goals. WHI has been for me a gateway to healthy and faithful aging. Thanks to the women in Group 105 of the Women's Health Initiative of the Nation's Capital, one of my current images of aging women is of *health pioneers.* Knowing that our work together is a gift to women of the future adds a lively sense of generativity to the undertaking.

The New Older Woman

A group of high-powered women over fifty met at a conference at the Esalen Institute in 1991, called by four of their number to discuss their own aging processes. Twenty-six women, among them anthropologist Mary Catherine Bateson, author Gail Sheehy, gerontologist Jane Porcino, and psychologist Cecilia Hurwich, shared ideas on staying energetic and productive after fifty, as well as their concerns about getting old. The women ranged in age from fifty-five to eighty-nine: five were in their fifties; thirteen in their sixties; six in their seventies; three in their eighties. The conversation among the women at the Esalen Institute is transcribed verbatim in *The New Older Woman: A Dialogue for the Coming Century*.

In addition to the ideas of these twenty-six women and how they age, Hurwich contributed the results of her own research of aging women, giving the reader a second layer of images. Echoing the conclusion of Hurwich's ten-year study of ten women over seventy, the major finding of *The New Older Woman* is that the way to maintain ongoing vitality is to identify your passion and pursue it.

Hurwich noted that the women in her study were all seriously involved in something outside themselves that was of compelling interest to them. All of them reached a point sometime in their fifties when they ceased their attempts to hang on to youth and looked forward to new possibilities. They prized nonconformity and cultivated eccentricity. Hurwich added that the women had friends of all ages, practiced good health habits, remained in their home, and stayed connected with world events. They also maintained a closeness with nature and liked gardening.

Believing that an interest in spiritual development is heightened in old age, I was both disappointed and puzzled that the women in *The New Older Woman* never mentioned their own spiritual or religious interests. Apart from a very few indirect references to religious background and ancient religious practice, the words *God, spirituality,* and *religion* had no place in their conversation. No one raised a question about the possibility of a transcendent spirit, let alone the existence of God. Apparently none belonged to a religious faith community, or if she did, that part of her life did not enter this conversation.

Perhaps these twenty-six women are thoroughly secular. Perhaps the churches, synagogues, and mosques are too patriarchal for them. This group of successful women of the world might illustrate what is called "the culture of disbelief." Culture dictates that religion is not to be taken seriously, even by those who profess a religious faith.[24] None of the Esalen women, however, gave evidence of religious belief. Then, too, perhaps philosophical or theological conversation was edited out of the published material.

I think too of Esalen participant Cecilia Hurwich's work with women over seventy. Were not any of these people, all passionately engaged in something outside of themselves, motivated by religious faith? If so, was the religious nature of the pursuit not worth mentioning at Esalen? It seems very strange that in a country where so many people identify themselves as religious believers that not one of these women had a religious perspective or used faith language in discussing her aging process. I struggle against creating yet another stereotype of the high-powered, successful older woman as thoroughly secular.

Conclusion

Stereotypes, like symbols, will always be around. There are stereotypes of two-year olds, of teenagers, of baby boomers, and of aged folks across that vast space called old age. Perhaps the stereotypes accurately define some of the people in the various age groups, but those persons ought not become symbols for all.

People create stereotypes, project what they will find, and then manage to meet their expectations. How does one avoid stereotyping others or being trapped in stereotypes themselves? An easier-said-than-done answer is to live in the present moment, open to one's deepest longing, open to the lure of God, open to novelty. Negative stereotypes can be avoided and positive images found to replace them. This is faithful aging.

For Personal Reflection

1. Ask three or four of people in your life to share their spontaneous thoughts about old age. A response to a question like "What three adjectives would you use to define old age?" might touch upon both attitudes and stereotypes.

2. What adjectives would you use to describe your current age group? What adjectives would you like to apply to yourself in old age?

3. How do you express your freedom? How do you share your wisdom?

4. Imagine that you are at an awards ceremony celebrating people who have successfully met the challenges life has handed them. You are among the survivors and "thrivors" to be awarded a badge. Whether you are middle-aged or old, design the badge that best describes the gift you bring to your family and to your community through your own surviving and thriving. Give your badge color, texture, and perhaps a title or brief message that summarizes the gift you offer.

5. What badges would you want to present to elders, living or dead, whose lives have enhanced your own?

Meditation

> *God's steadfast love endures forever,*
> *and God's faithfulness to all generations* (Psalm 100: 5).

Imagine yourself seated on a reviewing stand at the start of a parade. The people who will parade before you are adults who have been a significant part of your journey, going back as far as you can remember in childhood and coming right up to the present moment. Included are relatives and friends, school teachers, role models—people you have known personally. Also in the lineup are historical or literary figures whose lives have influenced yours for the better. Take your time to line up the people in the procession. . . . How do they look? What is your best guess as to how they most want to be seen? Attend to their facial expression. . . . As each one draws close to your place at the reviewing stand, she or he speaks a word to you. What do they say? . . . What would you like to hear? . . . What do you want to respond? . . . Let new images surface as they will.

> *God's steadfast love endures forever,*
> *and God's faithfulness to all generations.*

When the parade has ended, you are invited to join your circle of elders at a reception. . . . Walk among them. . . . Are you aware of common values they share? Are there words or images that would best describe your group of elders?

> *God's steadfast love endures forever,*
> *and God's faithfulness to all generations.*

Before the ceremony ends, stand or be seated in a circle with your elders and offer a prayer of thanksgiving for them. ... Does anyone add her or his voice to the prayer? ... How do you want to end the occasion?

God's steadfast love endures forever,
and God's faithfulness to all generations.

Further Reflection

Compare the images, words, and messages you received during the meditation with the stereotypical images and messages you hear about aging. How do you account for the difference? Do you have ideas about how you might contribute to increased respect for and incorporation of elders into a more age-inclusive, healthier society?

4

Looking Back with Insight

I admit to being on speaking terms with my past—with no guarantee of factual accuracy—and to using my memories as a source of inspiration and strength.

—Letty Cottin Pogrebin,
Getting Over Getting Older

THINKING PEOPLE INEVITABLY ASK these questions: Who am I? What do I feel called to do with my life? Is there a God? What will happen to me when I die? The thinking elder asks another question: how will I live until I die? Its answer will be shaped in large part by how one responds to the first four questions as well as by the person's health and financial resources. The answer will also depend on how a person has lived and what relationships constitute her or his present life.

When people are asked "Who are you?" typically they start with their name, a few identifying marks that locate them in the present—living status, occupation—and then they give a bit of history: where they were born and raised, significant stepping-stones along the way, perhaps a few accomplishments. Their answers imply, "I am who I am today, and my present has a history." This chapter is about that history:

how to review it, learn from it, reframe it, and reappropriate it. The process of recovering one's story starts when one speaks and is heard. Before discussing the power of listening, I begin with a reflective pause.

Reflective Pause

Take a moment to reflect on how you answer the question, "Who are you?"

The answer to "Who am I?" is never shared in full with another in this life. After the last breath, it's too late to tell anyone the very end of the story, and every moment of the story is a part of who I am. How can one convey to another what it was like finally to die, irreversibly to cross the great divide?

Human beings are always in process, always changing, always being shaped by the relationships that reveal to them who they are: relationships with themselves, with others, with nature, with God. Sharing their ongoing story with others is central to the process of becoming.

Listening and Being Heard

Genuine conversation takes two. I ask students in a counseling-skills course to recall a time when someone really heard them, a time when they spoke, uncensored, about something important to them, a time when the response from their listener was, "Tell me more." After pinpointing the occasion, they try to recover how they felt as a result of the conversation. Invariably the experience conveyed to them that they were important, deeply valued, fully alive, and perhaps both vulnerable and safe.

Assured of the goodness and trustworthiness of a conversation partner, people can risk allowing another to hear and see them for who they are. Students are also asked to recall a time when they offered caring, careful listening to another and to remember what happened in that process—to the other as well as to themselves.

Both telling one's own story to an absorbed listener and attentively hearing another's story are profoundly human experiences with lasting effects. It is as if a third reality enters the picture, a new creation. The third reality is the trusting relationship discovered or rediscovered in the telling and in the listening. The trusting relationship, present in the past, is a part of who one is in the present, and can be reexperienced with great satisfaction.

Memories and stories constitute a life. New York Cardinal Spellman was asked what motivated him faithfully to make regular Christmas visits to military service people around the world. He said he wanted to listen to them: "Every soldier has a story; every soldier is a story."

Stories capture the heart of life because from beginning to end every life is a story. Children often enjoy telling the same story over and over; generally they delight, too, in hearing parents repeat stories of adventure in their own childhood. Elders most relish telling their stories if responsive ears and hearts are ready to listen. I remember with regret and sadness an occasion when I offered physical assistance to a frail elder suffering with multiple disabilities. "Never mind that," she said as I arranged her food and drink. "Just sit down and talk to me." Many people helped her with very obvious physical needs. Few responded to her starvation for sharing stories—and most people did not find her easy to enjoy.

To "re-member" is to put the pieces or members back together. In the adult stage where integrity struggles with despair, remembering facilitates integration. Integrating one's never-ending story can be a rich blessing.

Some people flip their listening switch to its "off" position when an old person begins repeating a frequently told story or dwells on what may appear to be unnecessary details. Details deemed boring by some might be the very thing that makes the old person feel like a somebody. More significant than the recorded data about this individual's life—date and place of birth; social security number, driver's license, and passport numbers; employment record; age and sex of children—are the stories that convey her or his real identity. The underlying message is, "I want you to hear what you haven't really heard about me. Besides, I want to hear it as well. Please try one more time to really listen. You will help me accept myself as valuable. I must be more than all those unnecessary details that are part of my official record."

On a professional trip to Atlanta, I took advantage of a free afternoon to visit the Sadie G. Mays Nursing Home, founded after World War II by sociologist and concerned citizen Sadie Mays. This was the first nursing home open to African Americans in the South, a nonprofit institution funded by Medicare and Medicaid that houses over two hundred residents. At the time of my visit residents ranged in age from forty-seven to one hundred and four. The atmosphere at Sadie Mays is decidedly upbeat, open, and friendly. The one-story facility offers residents and their families easy access to well-kept grounds.

Two experiences most impressed me at Sadie Mays. First, scores of residents sit outside their doors and visit with one another. As if they were sitting on their front porches, they greet all who pass through the wide corridors. Pointing over her shoulder and into her "front door," one woman encouraged me go in and see her lovely, airy room with a view of the wooded grounds. "It's a beautiful room. It's my room—right there," she said with evident delight. Showing off her room to visitors increased her satisfaction. The "neighborhood" was friendly and welcoming. I did not see a "wheelchair wall" at Sadie Mays.

My second experience was meeting a woman I'll call Mrs. Cox. While waiting for an appointment with one of the administrators, I sat in the lobby where Mrs. Cox rolled her wheelchair close to the front door. She had immediate access to people entering and leaving. At the same time she was close enough to the front desk to keep up a running conversation with staff persons in the area. Mrs. Cox loudly proclaimed that she intended to collect pictures of all the residents in the home so that she could compile a photo history of Sadie Mays Nursing Home.

Dressed almost playfully in layers, Mrs. Cox wore a large curly wig and multiple tee shirts topped by a sweater; around her neck were perhaps a dozen necklaces of many colors. Listening to her disjointed snippets of conversation, I wondered if she was suffering from an early stage of Alzheimer's disease. When I moved to a chair close to her in order to greet her and introduce myself, she took the opportunity to tell me the wonders of Sadie Mays.

"This is a wonderful place—the best. Our meals are always served *on time*. We are given our medications *on time*." Pointing to the floor she said, "Just look how clean it is here. And our beds are changed two or three times a week, the walls dusted down."

"I feel like I've had a bath only when I use Dial soap," Mrs. Cox continued. When she moved into Sadie Mays, Dial was not sold in the nursing-home canteen. She prided herself in the fact that she convinced the home to carry her brand and buys the product frequently with her weekly allowance. "You couldn't find a better place."

Mrs. Cox's next story was about the Baptist church where she took two young boys for services many years ago. After giving several disconnected details about that particular Sunday, she got to the point of the story. One of the boys is now the senior pastor at the same large Baptist church in Atlanta. She discovered this on a Sunday morning when a friend picked her up at Sadie Mays to take her to services. To her great surprise, one of the men she introduced to the church as a boy appeared in the pulpit in his clerical robe. Apparently he was as surprised to see Mrs. Cox as she was to discover him in his new role. "He couldn't look at me without laughing," she said with a chuckle, "and when I went to receive Communion from him, he had to look away."

When I was summoned for my appointment and stood to leave, Mrs. Cox showed me where the canteen was located and suggested I check out the Dial soap. After my visit with the administrator and a heartwarming but sobering tour of the large facility, I reentered the lobby where Mrs. Cox was still holding forth. She saw me and began again, "I took two boys to church one day." Finishing that story she began, "I would like to get pictures of everyone at Sadie Mays. And since you visited us, I want to put your picture in our history book, too." I heard also about the availability of Dial soap. These are details that tell me who Mrs. Cox is; these are the fine points from her story that *she wanted to hear about herself.*

Why is remembering so pleasurable to elders, especially the old-old? Memories might compensate for multiple losses, assuring elders that all is not lost. Memories connect scattered parts of the puzzle into a unified picture, sometimes reconnecting people with a sense of wonder, delight, and engagement and keeping relationships alive. Vivid memories can yield a thick experience of the past, like images glimpsed through a wide-angle lens, and offer rich consolation. Remembering can rejuvenate the mind and inspire creativity.

Something even more significant is at work in remembering. Memories have the power to affirm one's worth, to give oneself a pat on the back. Generally people choose to recall their best selves, to bring to life the people with whom they shared mutually loving relationships. Memories tend to take people back to their favorite places and highlight their best accomplishments. With good memories brought to the forefront, one can judge one's life as good.[1] Not all memories are good, of course. Coming to peace with painful memories can be an important part of reclaiming a usable past.

Mrs. Cox's memory of her influence on two small boys was certainly a pat on her back. It also connected her with her church, her community, and her God. Lively engagement in the Sadie Mays world was evident in her storytelling. Obviously, she was proud that Dial soap was available in the canteen. Her interest in the history of the nursing home surely had a generative, creative flavor to it. She wanted the names and faces of residents to become a part of history, available for the next generation. And I was humbled and honored that she thought my picture might be included in that history.

Keeping alive treasures from the past is one reason why tools like *life review* are used with success by so many people. People need and want to own and share their histories in order to be solidly rooted in their world.

Life Review

The concept of life review, with a history in both Catholic and Protestant spirituality, was appropriated in the psychological literature in an article by Robert Butler. Butler claimed that universally elders are prone to review their histories, a need usually brought about by the realization of the brevity of one's life.[2] Encouraged by teachers, counselors, retreat leaders, and spiritual directors, life review has become a focused method of reminiscing that helps people of many ages to both gain an overview of their lives and pinpoint unresolved issues that cry out for resolution. Life review is not simply storytelling. It involves active grappling with one's past in order to make peace with it. Unresolved conflict plays a key role in the process. While life review deals with specific events in a person's history, the focus is not so much on the accuracy of detail as it is on the meaning and value of what happened.

Another advantage of life review is that it helps people discover the core narrative or central themes that provided an overarching structure to their lives. Families often have "party lines" or "topic sentences" that make up an ongoing story: "We were poor Irish immigrants." "My great grandparents were slaves." "My father ran away from home as a boy." "My ancestors fled Nazi Germany." "I did not know my birth parents," or "My parents wanted all boys." Some party lines highlight a fortunate family background, "We lived privileged lives," or "I had an ideal childhood." A whole narrative revolves around any one of these statements.

Life reviewers are empowered through the discovery, conflict resolution, and integration that retelling their story often entails, sometimes experiencing the whole process as religious atonement, at-one-ment, or coming to deep peace with one's life.

More psychological and philosophical than it is chronological, life review nonetheless uses chronology as a way of structuring the revisitation of the past. One looks back at major periods or stages in life in order to plumb their significance. Every structured attempt to answer "Who am I?" makes it possible to know oneself a bit more. Potentially, every revisit holds new insight. Generally people like to remember.

Remembering and Reconstructing the Past

Researcher Ellen Langer worked with seventy-five-year-old men who gathered for one week in 1979 at a country retreat. The men were taken back twenty years in their imagination. Magazines, books, music, and movies from 1959 were made available. "Thinking fifty-five," they spoke in the present tense. For seven days they had returned to fifty-five. As a result of the experience, impartial observers judged them to behave more fifty-five than seventy-five. Even more astounding, physiological measures indicated that "fingers straightened, stiff joints loosened, posture became more erect, hand grips grew stronger and IQ scores improved." Bones and muscles kept pace with self-perception.[3] Remembering and enacting the memories had definite therapeutic effects.

Clearly, looking back has been a major method in therapeutic practice. The past is relived, however, not for the sake of the past but for the sake of the present and the future. Unfinished business from the past, unexpressed pain and anger and grief need to see the light of day, so that the light of today might shine. Life review can supplement or sometimes replace the looking back that has or has not happened through a professional therapeutic relationship.

Some past memories bring immediate satisfaction, increasing one's faith and hope and appetite for life, and pointing to directions in which one would like to move. Some of the past, however, has been forgotten or repressed and is not available or usable in a helpful way. The painful past can be acknowledged and accepted as a part of the past. The power it exercises on the present can be taken back or reclaimed only if the past is accepted as one's history.

A person can be fully self-accepting only by accepting the fact that her history is her history, the good along with the bad. There is no way around it. Appreciation for the good lives side by side with sadness, disappointment, resentment about the bad. None of the emotions experienced in the present or the past need be repressed or rejected. Love along with hate, fear along with courage, joy along with sorrow— all are a part of the tapestry of one's life. Owning them does not mean acting on them. Owning all of one's experience makes a person more real, more integrated, more wise. Owning it all takes away the power of the past to blindly contaminate behavior in the present.

Does ownership imply acceptance? How can a person accept or befriend painful memories of rejection or abuse? To accept the undeniable fact that one's past is one's past, and therefore to own that past, does not mean to find all experiences in the past *acceptable*. To *accept* is to receive or acknowledge whatever is at hand. To judge something *acceptable* implies that it is worthy of being accepted. A note of approval is implied when one finds something acceptable, whereas accepting what cannot be denied does not require approval. The abuse or rejection experienced in the past is neither acceptable nor treasured. Abuse is despised and protested and grieved.

You treasure your life and the courage and stamina you found to survive threats to it. You treasure the fact that hope was not destroyed. You treasure the supportive relationships that helped you survive abuse. You treasure faith in a God who is always present, always luring human beings to choose life.

Some look back and are filled with guilt and regret over their abuse or neglect of others. Life review can facilitate their seeking forgiveness, from the other, from themselves, from God. What can be more freeing and life-giving than the belief that God forgives the past and that there is nothing one has to do about it oneself?

I contemplated this belief at the opening of a Sunday worship service. I came into the sanctuary a little downhearted, willing and needing to own with regret the unpleasant attitude I had inflicted on my husband during the previous days. I believed that I had to *do something* about it in order to be acceptable in God's presence. Then I knew I had to do nothing but open myself to God's love, accept and forgive myself, and move forward. I reached out and touched my husband's hand. What a grace!

Revealing Secrets from the Past

Buried secrets from the past can block life review. The secrets take on disproportionate power over people who are afraid to reveal them. Powerful secrets need to be shared carefully with interested, trustworthy others in whose presence it is safe to be vulnerable. Once the secret is revealed, however, the power can be broken, and the unburdened secret teller experiences a sense of relief and new psychic energy. For some, the immediate reaction is one of shame or regret. Why did I let others know this terrible truth? The secret tellers need reassurance of acceptance from those who heard their secrets before they feel empowered. Revealing a secret means that the energy spent on guarding the secret is now available for more profitable pursuits. Revealing a secret can lead to forgiveness of self and in many cases to forgiveness of one's offender. Revealing a secret can be a wonderfully liberating adventure.

It has been my experience as counselor that people who reveal a secret for a first time—and this can happen as early as the initial session—resolve the problem that they brought to counseling. Certainly further working through may be required, but the healing has begun.

Reframing the Past

One method used in therapy for working through troubling past experiences is reframing. To reframe an experience is to reconsider its impact and reinterpret its meaning. For example, in reworking a relationship with a deceased parent, reconstructing the parent's history can throw new light on the ongoing internal struggle the adult child has had with the internalized parent. Reframing happens when people discover their creative strengths through what they have survived. It also occurs when they are able to understand the other person in a way that makes her or his negative behavior or abuse of power more tolerable.

This happens outside formal therapy as well. For example, the adult daughter of a mother who had been frustrating (the daughter would say maddening) to live with, and about whom the daughter held extremely ambivalent memories, dialogued with her long-deceased mother. Using Ira Progoff's method of dialoguing, the woman imagined the stepping-stones of her mother's life. In doing so she listed the many losses that ended in her mother's prolonged but untreated depression. The daughter felt that she was able to walk in her mother's shoes before beginning the dialogue. The dialogue allowed the daughter to appreciate her mother as she never had before. Anger and resentment were transformed into sadness, empathy, understanding, and the beginning of a new relationship.

Ira Progoff's dialogue method, described in his book *At a Journal Workshop*, includes constructing the stepping-stones or critical events in the dialogue partner's life. The ensuing written dialogue can lead to a new understanding of the situational factors and the personality traits and behaviors that interfere with a satisfying relationship.

The internalized persons involved in troublesome memories are part of one's psychological environment in the here and now. Reframing can transform one's ongoing interior life with these internalized figures, sometimes converting adversaries into colleagues. A reframed memory results in a reframed relationship.

Survivors of abuse sometimes reframe the abusive relationship, focusing on their survival skills and strength of character rather than remaining trapped in the abuse. The violation is still seen as sinful and destructive. Feelings about the abuser may or may not change within the new frame; one's sense of self, however, changes.

There are many tools available for facilitating a life review, among them the lifeline and written dialogues. Clustering is also an excellent tool.

The Lifeline

A lifeline represents one's history from birth to anticipated death.[4] A horizontal time line is drawn across the center of a page, the year of birth marked on the left end, the current year at its appropriate place, and a dotted line extending beyond the solid line indicating the future years a person expects or desires to live. The projected year of death is written at the end of the dotted line.

As the person looks back over his life, he divides the years according to periods. These may coincide with progress through schooling: grade school, high school, college. Significant employment experiences or major family events may begin and end a period. Approximately seven periods are marked by vertical lines placed on the time line; each period is given a title.

On a separate piece of paper, a few key events in each of the periods are listed. Some may be peak experiences filled with religious significance; others, critical life passages laden with meaning. Some may be particularly difficult experiences that one survived.

In circles above the line, labels or titles are used to designate experiences remembered as positive and fulfilling. Beneath the lifeline, significant crises or difficulties are also given titles. Each circle is then tied like a balloon to the lifeline at its approximate time of occurrence. Once the lifeline is constructed, further possibilities for probing its significance emerge.

The Written Dialogue

Imagining your life as a spreading tree, a flowing river, or a winding road, you can see some of the events circled above and below the lifeline as major branching points in your life. Often gifts or talents that these events revealed are left untapped. A helpful way to recover or release the creative potential that the experience indicated is to dialogue with the event. The following steps lead a person into the dialogue.

1. Quietly return to the past when the event occurred. Recalling life at that time, list and then reflect on the people

who were important players in your world. Write adjectives describing these people and this period of life. What were your prevailing hopes and fears?

2. Allow the event to take on its own identity, to have its own voice. Note significant steps that led up to the event.

3. On a fresh sheet of paper, begin to dialogue with the event. Either of the dialogue partners initiates the conversation by asking: "How are things between us?"

4. Write out the full dialogue, just as it flows through the imagination. Using initials, note who is speaking as thoughts and feelings are exchanged.

You can revisit your lifeline over and over, with different events or persons engaged in a dialogue in order to develop further the gifts and possibilities still to be mined. Both resolving conflict in difficult past encounters and rediscovering the power of positive relationships make the past more usable.

Members of the extended family as well as close friends were undoubtedly involved in the circled events above and below the lifeline. There may be people in one's family of origin who did not surface in the branching points. It is worth reflecting on both those who did show up and those who were not there.

Perhaps the relationship with the person to whom one felt closest during childhood is most laden with possibility in the present. To discover those possibilities, one can use Gabriele Rico's method of clustering explained in chapter 3. Circle the person's name on the center of a page. Let words spill out all over the sheet, connecting words that seem to belong together, branching off when a new thought or feeling arises. When an "Aha!" breaks into consciousness, begin writing.

A next helpful step is a dialogue with this person and perhaps with other family members. Dialoguing with family members brings them to life in the present moment, making an ongoing spiritual relationship available, even with those who have died. It is important to spend some time briefly reconstructing the dialogue partner's life. What major stepping-stones marked her or his journey? What adjectives describe this person? Are you aware of ambivalent feelings toward the person?

After becoming quiet and focused for a few moments, begin a dialogue with either partner asking, "How are things between us?" or with the initiator saying, "I need to talk with you about _____." The conversation usually comes to its own good end.

Conclusion

The past covers all of a person's lived experience. How selective ought one to be in returning to an earlier stage of life? Some people easily discover what needs to be revisited, reactivated, and perhaps reinterpreted. The work proposed in the exercises at the end of this chapter will be most useful for persons who have a good memory of the significant events of their past life and have worked through any major difficulties they faced, such as rejection, abuse, or abandonment. People with little or no memory of their early years—from kindergarten and into grade school—are advised not to search for memories without the guidance of a trained counselor. Forgetting serves a purpose; uncovering can bring back repressed memories that require working through. Professional counselors and therapists are the best guides for such an endeavor.

For Personal Reflection

1. Assemble a collection of family photographs that you will keep before you as you work through these exercises. Spend some time reflecting on what you see and what you remember. Do you see anything you never noticed before?

2. Construct a timeline, mark the periods, and list key events within each period. Which of these experiences are vital to your story?

3. Are you aware of experiences in the past that you would like to better understand or see in a new light? If so, describe the experience in some detail. Who is involved? What impact did the experience have in the past? How does it influence your present life?

4. Choose one branching point that you sense holds untapped talent or resources for your present life. Using the suggested guidelines, dialogue with this event. If you are not able to converse with the event as if it were a person, you might try dialoguing with someone who was significant at the time of this event, again following the guidelines regarding stepping-stones in your dialogue partner's life.

5. Begin a clustering exercise by writing the name of a significant person from your timeline on the center of a piece of paper. After creating a web of words, anticipate an "aha," and when the inspiration comes, write. What do you learn about yourself through the writing? You may be aware of unhealed relationships in the past and uncover fresh memories of disturbing experiences. These can be revisited and reframed so that the power they have over you can be taken back and your past reclaimed in the process.

Meditation

Do not be afraid for I am with you.
Your past is my past. You are mine.

Return to an experience in your grade-school years that was especially satisfying . . . perhaps the happy memory of a time when you felt particularly good about life. Try to recreate the scene. . . . What season of the year is it? Notice who is present, what people are wearing, the expression on their faces. Take a good look at yourself. How do you look? Get into the feel of the day. Let the conversation unfold. . . .

Now imagine that it is your turn to speak to everyone in this setting. You feel fully in charge of what you want to say. You pause as you hear a voice inside say:

Do not be afraid for I am with you.
Your past is my past. You are mine.

And then you speak. . . . Stay with the scene as one or another person may want to respond to you. Let the conversation flow. . . .

Assume that there is a particular person in your life involved in this memory with whom you want to have a one-on-one conversation. Who is the person and how do you feel about your relationship to her or him? Ask this person to take a walk with you.

Do not be afraid for I am with you.
Your past is my past. You are mine.

The two of you find a favorite place and begin your stroll. What do you want to say? What do you want to hear? Let the conversation unfold. . . . Perhaps there will be silences, awkward moments when you don't know what you want to express. You don't have to say anything at all. Enjoy the quiet, peaceful place where you are walking. . . .

It is time for the two of you to part. What are your parting words to one another? Take your time to bid each other good-bye and include anything further you want to say. . . .

Now imagine that this person is here with you today. Look back together on where you were then and talk a bit about where you are now. What does your past say to you in the present? . . . End your meditation with a prayer, perhaps responding to the comforting words of God: *"Do not be afraid for I am with you. Your past is my past. You are mine."*

Further Reflection

If this meditation worked for you, you may want to reconnect with people in your past through a visit, a phone call, a letter, an exchange of photographs. Think of a next step you might take in bringing your past into the present.

5

Looking Forward with Vision

The only limit to our realization of tomorrow will be our doubts of today.

—*Franklin Delano Roosevelt*

IN CONCLUDING HIS LAST RADIO ADDRESS, to have been broadcast on Friday, April 13, 1945, the day following his death, President Roosevelt perhaps exaggerated when he declared that the only limit to our realization of tomorrow is our doubts of today. Some people struggle all their lives against unjust limits that follow the abuse of power through oppression. Racism, sexism, classism, and ageism limit all of those victimized by such systems. Alongside limitations imposed from outside the self, however, self-doubt is indeed self-limiting. Self-doubt has not found a usable past. Self-doubt does not live a satisfying present. Self-doubt does not project a promising future.

Unlike the future for a young person, which can feel like pure, unbounded possibilities, an aging person knows that the future will have real but limited possibilities. Most elders accept that they will never become concert pianists or professional dancers; they will never break seventy as golfers; they will never run for public office. All of them, however, can set realistic goals; most can look forward to satisfying experiences in the future.

Hope and Future Story

A promising future is about hope. I clustered the word *hope* after reading Andrew Lester's, *Hope in Pastoral Care and Counseling*. Hope is now wedded for me to Lester's challenging concept, *future story*, the often unarticulated ideas people carry in their imaginations about what their futures hold.

> Before, hope felt different to me. It meant believing, expecting, hanging on, living in faith, moving ahead, thinking positive, praying, trusting, waiting for a good outcome.
>
> Now hope has a different tone for me, a deeper yet quieter anticipating and believing, moving ahead with wide eyes and new intention, living positively, prayerfully, thriving within hope's promise, trusting, investing, translating hope into future story.
>
> "Age with vision, wisdom, and lots of zest," says Hope, "Don't wait, create. Age hopefully."

The difference between hope as I knew it in the past and present hope has to do with my intentionality about the future. Waiting has given way to creating. As a warm-up for a discussion of future story, you might try an exercise suggested by Lester.

Reflective Pause

Use a few moments to take inventory of how you spent your last waking day. List the things you did with your time. How future-oriented are the items on your list?

Human beings are people with agendas, agendas that involve what they plan to see happen or they fear will inevitably happen—sooner or later. Agendas pull them into their futures. While many people have not articulated what they project into their future, beyond how to pay next month's bills or perhaps how to spend the next holiday, such anticipation or dread is always at work in their unconscious minds and in their daydreams.

Children project themselves into the future. They say they will become doctors, firefighters, police officers, teachers, Olympic athletes. In disastrous environments, their imaginations can become tragic. In the midst of the Intifada, for example, Palestinian boys said they would be martyrs when they grew up; the girls would be wives of martyrs—so limited were their futures by their lived experience of war and death. Some teenagers and young adults have notions about the specific age at which they will die. People whose parents died before old age wonder if they will see more years than their parents did. Adult children of divorced parents sometimes live in fear and even expectation that their own marriages will come to the same end. Some adults have detailed stories about their own futures; they also project explicit expectations regarding their children's futures.

Hopeful future stories often assume a long and happy life, grandchildren and grand plans included. Reaching a desirable level of professional or financial success is central to many future stories and provides powerful motivation in the present. Making significant contributions to their communities through the investment of time, talent, and financial resources lures others into generous, generative living.

Possible selves are embedded in future stories. Possible selves are images or representations of the future self. They can be either real or ideal images of who you most want to become. They can also be frightening representations of what you fear you might become. Both hoped for and feared possible selves influence the self you are today.

The so-called midlife crisis combines a coming to terms with one's life cycle with the dilemma of an unrealized possible self in a failing future story. The possible self one had in mind did not quite materialize; the future story one hoped for somehow fell short. In retrospect, I know that my own midlife crisis and change was seven years in the making, the result of dramatic revisions in worldview: theological, psychological, and social. The future story that I believed and solemnly vowed would be my only future no longer pointed to health or happiness for me. With struggle, anguish, and grief, I moved from professed membership in a religious order in the Roman Catholic Church to single life with a view toward marriage. A very different future story involving a very different possible self took shape, one that has known challenge and deep satisfaction.

Future stories can be filled with magical thinking. Unrealistic childhood stories and self-deceptive adolescent stories need rewriting when adults recognize the futility of their projections and are converted to more realistic hopes. The longer people live, the more often the details of their future stories need to be revised.

The Loss of Future Story

Future stories are lost when a dream does not come true, when partners and loved ones die, when careers are disrupted, when fortune fails, when the aging process results in the loss of capacities. When a future story dies, a person must grieve. A new future story is needed to replace the old one. The loss of one story and creation of the next are at work simultaneously because both past and future are alive in one's imagination, consciously and unconsciously. As one works through the grief process, one must be alert to magical thinking that can shape a dysfunctional future story in the wake of loss. Whether optimist or pessimist, a grieving person can attempt to move into new possibilities too fast or find it impossible to move at all. A person in grief needs the careful listening of a wise friend or counselor in redesigning a future story that integrates past and present realities with future hopes and dreams.

A large challenge in old age is to resolve the struggle between *integrity* and *despair*. There are many roads to despair. The loss of future story contributes to despair. Reaching the end of a future story without replacing it with new aspirations can lead to despair. Being buried in the present, incapable of imagining new possibilities, eventuates in despair. The inability to find a usable past or to claim a satisfying future results in a person being present-bound, living with a sense of defeat and despair. Enmeshment in a finite future story, one that comes to a dead end, leads to meaninglessness and despair. Negative images of a punitive god can lead to despair. Looking at death and seeing nothing beyond but void can bring some to despair.[1]

Although I am a person who wants and needs to see beyond the void, who wants and does believe in an infinite God on the other side of finite human life, I know people who do not share my wants, needs, or beliefs. I have relatives and friends who do not believe in God, who do not believe in an afterlife, and they have not despaired. They need no conviction about anything beyond this life to find meaning and hope in their life now. Motivated to make something of their lives and to contribute to the well-being of their families and communities, they live hopefully. Those who do believe in personal immortality, with the expectation that they will find fullness of life, have increased motivation to live hopefully.

A future without hope is a dreadful future, surely not worth striving for. One expects more of the same, becoming stuck in repetitious patterns from the past. The way out of the vicious cycle is through relationship. If a hopeful person can be present to a hopeless person in honest relationship, hope is alive in at least one half of the relationship, keeping despair at bay.

Future stories often neglect the reality of age. They tend to highlight the longed-for accomplishments of adulthood, but include little about elderhood. "I want to be a doctor when I grow up" doesn't include what the doctor does when she or he retires. "We will pay loans for our children's education and then retire" does not include how the couple will live their retirement years. Some future stories go further. "I'll live to see my grandchildren marry" pushes the adult into retirement years. And then what?

The task for elders is to articulate their future stories, always open to dreaming larger dreams. The question is, how much longer does one need to live in order to make a future story worthwhile? If an elder knew that she or he had ten years to live, would they craft a future story? What about five years? Three years? One year? People with catastrophic illness are sometimes willing to undergo excruciating treatment if they think they might have an extra year or two to enjoy. They choose to fight to live. Others struggle with an incurable illness and reach a point where they are ready to say their good-byes and let go. The following stories illustrate how two elders handled their future stories. The first introduces a woman who made a courageous decision that brought new adventure into her life; the second is about a man who told large future stories about both living and dying.

Future Story Illustrated

For as long as she could remember, Catherine Pacheco suffered a water-related phobia that made it difficult for her to sit on a docked vessel, much less take to the sea. Her husband's interest in sailing, coupled with her favorable impressions of colleagues with a passion for the water, convinced her that she wanted to overcome her handicap. Using self-directed behavior modification, she began taking sailing expeditions with friends, and step by step over several years of effort became both a sailor and a swimmer.

Pacheco reported a spectacular day and night on the *Romany Star,* the 38-foot sailboat she and her husband lived on for over ten years. Her husband resting below deck, Pacheco took charge. She kept watch for boats approaching in the darkness, adjusted pulleys that worked the tiller, and reveled in the magnificence of the evening. White sails filled with fresh wind gleamed in the starlight as the *Romany Star* flew through the sea. Pacheco was aware of another journey—the journey she courageously took from her handicapped, fearful life to one of new possibilities. She returned to her huddle in the cockpit and came to a sobering realization: had she not decided to break her phobic fear of water and search for new patterns in her life, she would have missed this night. She realized how much she might have lost.[2]

While the task of shaping a future story becomes more difficult for people who live into their nineties without good health, there are trailblazers who never stopped being and doing and planning as they continued to live out a future story, whether with weakened or strong hearts and limbs.

At age seventeen, hypnotherapist Milton Erickson gradu-ated from high school. That same year he was stricken with polio and was totally paralyzed; the doctor believed his death was imminent. Erickson survived and lived a full life as husband, father, grandfather, teacher, and noted clinician. He spent the last six years of his life meeting daily with groups of psychotherapists interested in learning more about his therapeutic method. Erickson used teaching tales both in his therapy and in his teaching. A tale about father and son is entitled "On Death and Dying." It is also about life and living and the future story that lured these two men to extend their lives.

The story was motivated by a worried student who feared that Erickson was dying, an idea that Erickson told him he believed was entirely premature. He let the student know that he had no intention of dying. "In fact, that will be the last thing I do!"

Erickson's mother lived until she was ninety-four; his grandmother and great-grandmother lived beyond ninety-three. His father died at ninety-seven after a fifth heart attack. Each time the prognosis for his father was grim; each time his father mocked the doctor's predictions. When told once that he needed two or three months to recover, his father replied, "Two of three months, my foot! What you mean is I've got to waste a whole week!" One week later he was home.

His father planted fruit trees within the year of his death, wondering if he would be around to enjoy the fruit. At ninety-seven, Erickson's father planned a weekend trip with two of his daughters. All details in place—where to stay, whom to visit, which restaurants to frequent, the three trav-elers walked out to the car. The father returned to the house to pick up a forgotten hat. After a considerable wait, his daughters intuitively knew what had happened and went into the house where they found their father dead of a massive cerebral hemorrhage. Milton Erickson concluded this story by advising people to enjoy life thoroughly with as much humor as possible. As for the student's query, he said that he didn't know where the student got the idea that he was going to die. Erickson fully intended to put that off.

At age seventy-eight, Milton Erickson finished a regular teaching week on a Friday; early Sunday morning he stopped breathing. A future story was complete.[3]

Retirement and Future Story

The network losses that follow retirement were discussed in chapter 2. The emphasis here is on the possibilities that open up once the losses have been faced. Now what?

Faithful aging means reframing retirement as a time of renewal. Belonging to the young-old anticipating the end of full employment, I clustered the word *retirement* and wrote:

Retire.
Re-tire.
Four new all purpose tires . . . and a spare.
Satisfaction guaranteed.
Let the wheels roll, roll, roll.
I will roll my way into retirement.
A lengthy spin with lots of time to play along
    the roads not yet taken.
Blue highways.
A time to think long thoughts up and
    down the ribboned road.
A time to plan more rolls down still other lanes not taken.
Re-tire is wise rebirth.
Happy birthday.

Perhaps the major problem people have with retirement is that they feel ill-prepared for it the morning after the long anticipated celebration. They have not written a new future story, and the dreams and narratives that brought them to the point of retirement are outlived, dissatisfying, or simply not available. Many retirees are left in a vacuum. People who have not developed interests and hobbies outside their occupation will struggle to know what to do with themselves. They resemble the man ambling through the house from room to room, distraught, without a clue as to how to use his abundance of time.

For those living in marriages or committed partnerships, the changes that retirement brings affect each person *and* their life together. When both members of the partnership are ending employment outside the home, the change in the system can be even more dramatic. Whether retiring at the same time or separately, each must change as the system they created to structure their lives together changes.

Successful retirement requires a conversion—a turning away from the familiar in order to embrace a new life with a different future. Believing that the word *retirement* has negative connotations that emphasize isolation and diminishment rather than choice and creativity, elders have suggested alternative titles: recommencement, renaissance, the elective years, reengagement. All of these preferred titles point to an expansive future story.

Constructing a Future Story

Unlike stories from the past, the future story is long on hopes and dreams or fears and dreads, but short on detail. It isn't easy to "tell" a story about a future that is not here yet, but concrete ideas about what the future will and will not hold often live deep beneath the surface of people's conscious minds. Intentionally thinking and planning a future story adds challenge and anticipation to life in the present. Details make it more likely that a future story will materialize.

While some good things in life simply fall into people's laps, more often they work hard to achieve what they want to accomplish. Realizing a future story takes the same kind of effort.

Reflective Pause

Recall a time when you wanted something very badly, worked hard to make it happen, and enjoyed the results of your efforts. You could probably outline how you strategized to reach your goal, listing steps you took that brought you closer and closer to the finish line. What was the best thing you did to achieve your goal? Planning a future requires such strategies.

First, you must use your imagination to envision in detail what you want your coming years to look like. With a vision in place, you then can outline the steps you need to take in order to realize your dream.

A helpful way to begin to construct a future story is to imagine what you would like your life to look like in ten years, then describe it in as much detail as you can imagine. Another way to get concrete about the future story is to write a list of things you want to do before you die. Each of these exercises is described at the end of the chapter.

Conclusion

People are not unconcerned or mindless about the future. Future thinking is happening all the time. Seminars are offered by financial institutions eager to help middle-aged and older people plot their financial futures. Wanting to hold a measure of control over the health decisions that will be made in their regard, more and more people are writing living wills and durable powers of attorney. Announcements from real-estate developers eager to help elders with financial means to settle into their next residence regularly are deposited in mailboxes. Retirement communities across the country offer a wide selection of lifestyles, often with the emphasis on leisure pastimes such as golf, water sports, and arts and crafts. The commercial world broadcasts with annoying frequency the advantages of food supplements and sanitary products for the aging.

What is missing from most of these goods and services is recognition of the higher level needs like intergenerational belonging, meaningful engagement, spiritual yearnings, and service to others. The emphasis is seldom on leaving a legacy of faith and hope and love for those who follow. What is missing is the notion of a full and generative future story.

For Personal Reflection

1. Picture yourself as you would like to appear ten years from now, in whatever setting you prefer. Then consider these questions:

What three adjectives best describe this image of yourself?
Who are your friends?
Describe your primary relationship(s)?

What do you feel most passionate about and how does it show up in your central activities?

Describe your career or volunteer commitments.

How do you spend your leisure time?[4]

How do you express your generativity or care for the generations?

2. List thirty things you want to do before you die. Such a list stimulates values clarification and lends itself to rewriting a future story. It also makes it more likely that you will do some of these things. After constructing your list, put a check mark next to the things that would be more realistically accomplished than others. Go back over the list, marking the top ten items on your list. Next prioritize these ten, with number one your highest priority. How will you move forward from here?

Does your list give clues about your future story? You might keep this list, date it, and review it every six months. When you accomplish items, date their accomplishment and add something new to the list so that there are always thirty things yet to do before you die.

3. Pay attention to the hidden future stories implied in print and electronic advertisements involving elders. What values are highlighted?

4. Consider how your own future story has changed since you reached adulthood. Are there aspects of that story that have endured?

5. Write a paragraph that captures your future story today.

Meditation

When you send forth your Spirit, we are created;
with you we renew the face of the earth (Psalm 104:30).

Imagine that you have been given a full year to pursue whatever you want to experience or learn, with all expenses paid. There are no barriers: you can go anywhere, do whatever you want. What would be the most fulfilling way you could use the time? What would you most want to accomplish?

If you choose, all of your responsibilities at home and work could be handled by other people. If you wish to spend all or part of the time away from home, you can take others with you, all expenses paid. You are free to use whatever means of transportation you prefer. There are no limits to educational opportunities, personal or professional enrichment, work or travel possibilities during the twelve months. You can move about as often as you wish. Take several minutes to think about how you want to spend your year. . . . What do you want to accomplish?

When you send forth your Spirit, we are created;
with you we renew the face of the earth.

Several months into the year, you decide to review what the time has meant to you. Sit down with a trusted friend and talk about your experience. Would you like to make any changes in your plans? If so, what do you want to add? What do you want to forgo? What are you learning about yourself in the process? Make any changes that might add meaning and value to your year off. . . .

When you send forth your Spirit, we are created;
with you we renew the face of the earth.

Let your imagination roam, and live through your days and weeks, engaged in your world, moving into the immediate future. . . . Although you may have months left to enjoy this wonderful year, in a few moments you will return to the group and talk about your experience. Take one last minute to come to a pause in your adventure. . . .

When you send forth your Spirit, we are created;
with you we renew the face of the earth.

Further Reflection

This meditation may have opened new possibilities for your future story. Look back over the answers you gave to the questions raised at the end of this chapter in light of the meditation you have just made. Is there anything you want to add to the paragraph on your future story?

6

Valuing the Present

If life becomes dull and routine and we're tempted to admit that we're feeling the impact of aging, there'll be no doubt as to the fact that it's time to make a change. But as long as every day is exciting and challenging, as long as what we're doing keeps us young and healthy . . . we won't have to go searching for the right pattern . . . we'll know that we're squarely in the middle of it.
—Catherine Chapman Pacheco,
Breaking Patterns: Redesigning Your Later Years

HAVING LOOKED BACK AND RECLAIMED A usable past, looked forward and projected possibilities for the future, you are left to decide what to do now—how to enhance the value of life in the present. The present encompasses many things. Foremost perhaps is good-enough health, without which life can be a suffering burden. Life in the present encompasses a typical daily or weekly agenda: meals, rest and exercise, work and play, solitude and interaction, service to others, engagement in the community, reading, study, prayer, and worship. The frequency and quality of relating to others dramatically determines the character of life in the present. Well-connected people have more enriched and satisfying lives than people who are isolated and enjoy few if any intimate relationships. On the spiritual level, the frequency and quality of centering oneself before God determines the character of one's connections, as well as the depth and breadth of one's life in the present.

Catherine Pacheco suggests indicators for assessing satisfaction with your present life. Is everyday life exciting and challenging? "Engaging" might be a more useful word than "exciting"; engagement includes the use of your gifts and talents and involvement with others. Generativity, a still more significant indicator, must be added to the equation. The question is whether you are making a difference to others through care, concern, and efforts to improve the quality of life in the community. Or you might look at life from the end: If this were the last week of your life, how would you want to spend it?

A consistently exciting and challenging life may be unrealistic. The hope of remaining "*young* and healthy" is surely wishful thinking. Obviously, there are normal everyday struggles, disappointments, and setbacks, and although the old may be quite healthy, they do not become young again. Nonetheless, considering life as a whole, do you feel physically, emotionally, and spiritually healthy and generally engaged and challenged? If not, it is time to consider a change.

A helpful way of assessing life in the present is to ponder your needs and values. This chapter explores the origin and development of values. Values clarification is used to determine whether what you say are cherished values do in fact function as values in your day-to-day life. Finally, the values of elders are discussed, concluding with the value of religious faith and institutional religion. The first question is, what constitutes a value?

Values

A value is anything considered important to the good life. Values are divided roughly into *instrumental values* (means to an end) and *terminal values* (states of being or ends). *Care* and *honesty* illustrate instrumental values; *justice, equality* or a *world at peace* are examples of terminal values. The concept of values underlies much of everyday speech. People choose what to care about, talk about, work for, worry about. They choose their values.

Hierarchy of Values

Psychologist Abraham Maslow, using the words *need* and *value* interchangeably, distinguished between what he called *deficiency* needs or values and *growth* needs or values. Deficiency values are lower-level needs. Everyone requires the same basic commodities: food and water, sleep and exercise. When necessities such as nourishment and shelter, safety and security go unmet, people are not free to yearn for growth values such as truth or justice. Their energies are consumed by the urgency to stay alive and protect themselves from harm. If basic needs or values go unmet for too long, a person will have a distorted value system with insatiable cravings for acceptance, security, connection, and love that can never be satisfied.

Basic needs or values are blocked in old age for those with inadequate financial resources to obtain sufficient food, shelter, and health care. Safety and security needs are blocked when people live in excessive vulnerability or without assurance that they can care for themselves or be cared for in their future. Belongingness needs are obstructed through disrespect or neglect by family, friends, or neighbors, as well as by the institutional isolation of elders in age-segregated living. The interdependent needs for self-esteem and esteem by others are threatened whenever an old person is cast off or isolated from family or community. Self-esteem suffers also when a person is not afforded adequate privacy or a sense of control over her or his daily life. Once these needs are met, growth needs and values emerge.

The growth values are higher level needs, virtues like truth, goodness, beauty, and justice. A person whose foundational needs are satisfied is drawn toward a higher-level value and makes vocational and lifestyle choices based on that. In other words, human beings have their own value systems, hierarchical in structure, with one or two core values shining above the rest. A person whose overriding passion is justice will perceive the world differently from a person whose pivotal passion is beauty. Their responses to oppression and to visual offensiveness will vary, as well as the actions they take in the absence of justice and beauty.

Clusters of Values

Values tend to come in clusters or bunches like grapes. It is not always easy to distinguish one value from another.[1] To say that a person values relationship, for example, suggests the appreciation of many kindred values: honesty, trust, love, fidelity, community, connection, closeness, engagement. Genuinely to strive for peace assumes the valuing of care, justice, community, right relationship. The question then is how to locate or distinguish a core value, or the central values around which many values cluster. The following questions help a person locate her or his cluster of values.

What makes you deeply happy?
What makes you very angry?
What wounds or hurts do you resent having suffered?

What talents or gifts were you given for which you are most grateful?

Who are or have been your important role models and what values do they demonstrate?

What enhances your self-esteem?

What depresses you?

What do you daydream about?

When does your body feel most alive, most energetic, least apt to be tired?

What beliefs would you find it impossible to give up?

What jobs, tasks, assignments come your way without your asking for them?

What do you want to see unfold in your future?

Answers to these questions point to needs and values that may or may not be active in a person's life. After tracing the origin and development of values, a process for discerning when a value is operative will be discussed. In the questions at the end of the chapter, readers will be asked to return to the above questions and put their values to the discernment test.

The Origin and Development of Values

Values have a life history. They take root in childhood and develop over a lifetime. Children are taught their parents' values, values not yet freely chosen, by what parents say, and more effectively, by how parents behave. Growing up in a family is an education in values, both honorable values and selfish values. Some of these values extend over the lifetime of the child turned adult. Others are left behind when the child reaches maturity.

Reflective Pause

What values were held in your family of origin, and what behaviors followed? What values did you cherish in your earlier adult life, and what behaviors followed? What do you most value as an elder, and what behaviors follow? Consider the similarities and dissimilarities among the answers you give to the three questions. What do you learn from the exercise?

In addition to family as shaper of values, culture and society, socioeconomic status, race, education, and sex influence what one prizes. Values are transformed or replaced in adolescence and adulthood when one either reappropriates family values or replaces them.

For example, orderliness, which clusters with the values of control and discipline, might have been a central value in one's childhood home. Because of an excessive emphasis placed on the value, and serious consequences when the value was not upheld, emancipated young adults may relish the freedom to live in total clutter. Disorder is not the new value; freedom of self-expression is the value, and the right to live in chaos demonstrates that freedom. Unless the rebel lives alone, however, or finds a partner with a need for similar self-expression, the disorder will probably play havoc in the life of someone else, limiting the other's freedom and making relationships difficult.

In another case, family love and loyalty may be valued in a family from generation to generation. With few exceptions, grandparents, parents, and children all become symbols of hospitality and friendship among themselves and within their social circles. It becomes second nature to people nurtured in this family to open their homes and hearts to one another and to outsiders. Through the generations, the homes of members of the extended family become places where people of all ages like to congregate.

Values tell a person who she or he is. Clarifying and expressing core values results in a more solid sense of self, a feeling of integrity, as well as a stronger awareness of purpose and direction. By the time people becomes elders, they might be quite clear about the core value or values that focus their lives, knowing when their values are evident and when they are in jeopardy. The task for them is to find ways in which the growth values can be maximized. Other elders might not be as clear about what they most value in their present life, or they may have lost the ability or the habit of living their values. Still others raise new questions about life and death, free choice and social responsibility; value questions seen as more academic in the past are now felt as urgent.

Your values may describe the way you *wish* things were rather than the way they are; values may reflect the perceptions of others rather than the way you experience yourself. When are values really values? If a value is not evident in a person's life, is it an authentic value? While values are always in process, always in transition, there are ways of determining which values truly ground one's life. We can also discern the movement of God's Spirit in value-based decisions.

Values Clarification

Adolescents undergo a whirlwind of changes—physical, emotional, relational, spiritual—and end up confused about their values. They are at a crossroads where both family and social values are put to the test, sometimes suspended or replaced by what the adolescent chooses as a preferred way of living.

Elders are at another crossroads—perhaps quite clear about what they value, but reconsidering which values outweigh others, and trying to decide what is worth pursuing and where energies might best be spent. "How will I live until I die?" is a value-laden question. Elders can benefit from both the clarification of long-held values and the development of new or latent ones, in order to enhance their lives in the present.

The values clarification question is, when is a value an operative value? When is something that is perceived as a good truly at work in a person's life? Seven criteria can determine if a stated value is in fact a working value: 1) a value is chosen from *among alternatives*; 2) the alternatives are *thoughtfully considered*; 3) the value is *freely chosen*; 4) the value is *prized and cherished*; 5) the value is *publicly affirmed*; 6) the value is *acted upon repeatedly*; 7) such action becomes a *pattern* in the person's life.[2] In other words, genuine values result in predictable habits and behaviors.

The Needs and Values of Elders

A Personal Hierarchy of Values Illustrated

In contrast to Catherine Pacheco's suggestion that the words *dull* and *routine* belong together, other elders highlight the need for good habits or *routines*, a value writer May Sarton believed essential to peaceful aging. Routine provides a structure that gives people a sense of control over their lives and a sense of order within it. Sarton likened a day without a steady routine to a body without bones, calling it "a limp impossible mess." A related need for *order* and distress over disorder are themes woven throughout her journals, illustrating the origin and development of a personal hierarchy of values.

Sarton was moved from home to home, country to country during her early years in Europe, at times without one parent and then away from the other, and with little sense of control over her space. As an adult she highly valued order and routine. She was constantly aware of a quantity of unanswered mail, no matter how consistently, even compulsively, she responded to letters. The disorder of her desk, laden with letters from friends and admirers, was both terrifying and disorienting. Sarton elevates and generalizes the importance of both external and internal order, saying that *what life is all about* is the remaking of order in as simple a task as cleaning up after a meal. While most people do tend to clearing the table and washing dishes, she believed, few attend to the "dishes" of the inner world of feeling and thinking. As a result of the disarray, people living in inner chaos become exhausted and ill.[3] People without the same need for control and order might consider Sarton's need obsessive and even find a measure of inner disarray to be creative. The next vignette illustrates how a long-held value was replaced.

The Transformation of Values

A woman attending a conference on retirement illustrated the transformation of values in her life as she moved into late middle-age. Married to an ordained minister and living in a parsonage throughout their ministry, she decided with her husband to build their dream house for retirement—the first house they would own. The new home became a centerpiece in their future story. Along with the core value of religious faith, they valued security, comfort, and beautiful surroundings and sought to establish these values for their future life. The woman attended to every detail of their perfect home; the house was beautiful and gave the couple great satisfaction.

As property values escalated remarkably over the years, however, taxes increased, and the couple could no longer afford to maintain their dream home. They had to sell. She simply could not call a real estate agent. Instead, she studied real estate, secured her license, and served as her own agent. Prior to selling the property, she created a ritual and went from room to room in the home, grieving her loss. Taking note of the exquisite detail she had so carefully executed, prayerfully she let each room go. She also made a major decision that has influenced her life since the sale of the dream home. She lives in the present moment and is unwilling to put much energy into planning for tomorrow. The value of living in the present moment increased; physical comfort and control over the future decreased. Nonetheless, she did attend a conference on facing retirement.

Core Values of Elders

All of the new images of aging gleaned from the writings and words of elders and discussed in chapter 3 are value laden. The values include freedom, generativity, vital engagement, learning, and health. While relationship was implied in these values, the importance of mutual relationship is so central to satisfying aging that it warrants further exploration.

I find myself walking around with a new consciousness, perceiving elders in a different way than I did only a year ago. What I experience with increased intensity is the need of elders for genuine connection with all age groups. Befriending people of many ages expands horizons and increases one's capacity for empathy and generativity. It also helps people accept their place in the life cycle.

While the old may cherish good relationships, too often they feel shoved aside, outside the sphere of activity and interest of younger people with whom they would like to enjoy rich connections. Treated with indifference by those around them, they do not feel loved. Admittedly it takes two to develop a relationship. Surely part of the responsibility of staying connected, loving and seeking love, rests with the older adult: faithful aging requires initiative in developing and sustaining relationship. Responsibility also lies with people of all ages being caring and generous in seeking contact with their elders.

A wish list composed by centenarians includes such things as the desire for better awareness of the elderly and better communication among generations; a longing that the old be included and not relegated to the background; the yearning for elders to be needed and wanted, loved and accepted; the hope that families would care for their older members so that the old could live at home and not in nursing homes; the wish that the incapacitated were visited more frequently, and that the phone would ring more often.[4]

Sometimes elders contribute to their isolation. For example, when people call attention to the fact that they are old enough to be someone's parent or grandparent, limits may be put on the dialogue and potential relationship. In my work as teacher, I have developed remarkably rich friendships with students that continue over years, even decades. Were I to focus on the fact that I am old enough to be their mother, and now for some to be grandmother, the mutuality we experience in the relationships could diminish. I am well aware of the age difference, yet within conversation with these people, we often become peers.

A similar process can be true in the lives of grandmothers and grandfathers. They are more than a role to their grandchildren, as well as to others who are generations younger. It is one thing to be quite aware of age difference, another to fall into a way of thinking that overemphasizes chronological age, even ruling out the possibility for genuine mutuality when an age difference is significant.

Listen to theologian Henri Nouwen's understanding of how the elderly, through the attention of younger friends, might rediscover the wisdom of the child in a second playfulness.

> To care for the elderly means to play with the elderly in the hope that by playing together we will remind each other that dancing is more human than rushing, singing more human than shouting orders, poetry more human than *The Wall Street Journal,* and prayers more human than tactful conversations.... This can include walks to rediscover nature, poetry to rediscover words, music to rediscover sounds, and prayer to rediscover God.[5]

The young engaging the old in play illustrates generativity from the younger generation to the older. In the process younger people discover the wisdom of age and discover themselves, present and future, in the process. Such interaction could replace the stereotype of the old-old parked in senior centers where play is unimaginative, television programming banal, and activity reduced to assembly-line or routine tasks. Where are the players, dancers, musicians, nature lovers, poets, and pray-ers—the spirited playmates who might reintroduce the old-old to the wisdom of the child, help them discover a second playfulness, and in the process develop mutually enriching relationships?

Elders value family; elders value friends. While relationships with family members are significant to elders, research indicates that friends are more important to their psychological well-being. Older adults have known their closest friends for an average of 23–39 years; their less close friends, 19–24 years.[6] As important as family members can be to a sense of belonging and affection, knowing that others, unrelated by blood, have freely chosen to share life over the long haul gives a person a sense of acceptance, purpose, and deep connection. The need and desire for friendship and intimacy crosses age, gender, race, and class. Ultimately all genuine values are associated with relationships—with self, with others, with the transcendent. The happiest elders I know are playful people who love and are loved by friends of all ages.

When elders live within a religious framework and participate in a faith community, their core values can be transfused with a sense of the holy. What follows is a discussion of the value of religious faith and institutional religion, and of the needs religious community can meet in the lives of elders.

The Value of Religious Faith

The word *religion* implies that human beings are linked to Ultimate Reality. Women and men have the spiritual power to transcend themselves and reach for the absolute; religion intimates that the Transcendent is revealed and can be discovered and grasped in this life. Religion, however, is more than awareness and connection through personal contemplation. People not only glimpse the Transcendent, they can pursue the values of the Holy and pattern their lives on what they believe to be attributes of Ultimate Reality—values such as goodness and love, openness and gift of self. Expression of one's awareness and convictions through corporate worship and social concern make religion real and active, an indication that it is a functional value in the day-by-day, week-by-week life of the religious person. An endless variety of forms of expression account for the incalculable number of religions in the world.

The benefits elders receive through their religious faith

and spiritual life are awesome. If faith is not a gift from God, then it must be a human creation. Even if that were the case, and I don't believe it is, religious faith would be worth manufacturing because its power and advantages are central to the life satisfaction of many. Look at the statistics. Seventy-five percent of Americans over sixty-five say that religion is very important. In the Southeastern United States, the numbers rise to almost 90 percent. More than half of older Americans attend church or synagogue weekly or more often. A study of attendees in a geriatric assessment clinic revealed that over 50 percent of the patients reported that nearly all or all of their closest friends were from congregations.[7]

Why is a life founded on religious faith appealing and satisfying to so many elders? The simplest answer is that God is appealing, satisfying, and available to all. Surely the fact that people in the fourth quarter of their lives are closer to death leads to more frequent questions about the meaning of life and curiosity about what is on the other side. Beyond that natural concern, elders usually live under less day-to-day pressure and have more time to read and reflect on philosophical and religious questions. Old age is a fruitful time for spiritual interest and development.

Another obvious reason why faith is satisfying to so many elders is that it works. Religious faith can yield an experience of the most profound acceptance and love; religion also offers forgiveness for past sins and shortcomings.

The process of forgiveness ought not be oversimplified. Forgiveness within human relationships takes time. Offended people need to express the pain of betrayal, rejection, or abuse in the presence of their offenders, and the offenders need to communicate responsibility and sincere regret for what they have done. In many cases, the offender is not available for such conversation, either psychologically or physically, and the process must take place through communication with a sensitive listener—a friend, a therapist, a minister. For the believer, God is a part of the whole process; in God's presence, forgiveness is given and received.

Accepting God's forgiveness for past failings requires time as well, but only as much time as it takes for a person to forgive him- or herself and receive the grace of God's forgiveness. There are few things more powerful than knowing that one is forgiven, whether the forgiveness comes from a partner in relationship, from oneself, or from God. To know forgiveness is to experience fresh energy for a fresh start.

Religion also helps people recognize the blessings in their lives and live gratefully. A spirit of gratitude leads to a more profound acceptance of one's life cycle and lessens the tendency to compare one's circumstances with others. Perhaps all people might benefit from reciting a litany of gratitude as they greet each day. I am reminded of a friend who received a heart transplant after years of critical health, including near death experiences, and very poor prognoses. He awoke the morning after his transplant surgery filled with pure joy and gratitude. But why wait until surviving a major crisis to be grateful?

Studies have shown a relationship between religion and mental health in later life. People who value religion tend to suffer significantly less depression, are less likely to be mentally impaired, and less likely to use alcohol. They report that they enjoy strong social support. Hospitalized older women who identified themselves as religious recovered sooner and were less depressed than nonreligious peers in the same general hospital. Asked what contributed to their longevity, the most common responses from a group of patients were physical and mental activity, a strong belief in God, "Christian living," and a positive attitude toward self and others.[8] Religion enhances life.

Active engagement in religious activity with others heightens the positive effects of religious belief. The social engagement involved in corporate worship, for example, renders it more effective than private devotion. Studies support a positive correlation between church participation and participation in other areas of life at all ages, as well as a correlation between good personal adjustment and church attendance. Either the well-adjusted participate in religious activities or these activities contribute to their adjustment. For obvious reasons active participation in religious activities outside the home decreases with advanced age, but private religious expression increases for those who are no longer able to participate actively in church or synagogue.[9]

The added benefits of social engagement in a community of faith underscores the importance of members of congregations staying in frequent contact with older adults who can no longer come to the place of worship. Especially for ill and frail elderly and for the old-old, faith in God and connection within a community helps maintain a sense of identity and significance, keeps hope alive, sustains a sense of purpose when physical capacities are shutting down, and brings comfort and joy when one is most in need.

Religious values shift from doing to being as a person approaches frail old age. *Being* requires only attending to the present moment, finding peace and contentment in oneself, in one's faith, in simple pleasures. A seventy-nine-year-old priest who has found such peace calls his passage into a new stage in life the promotion from "plum-easy doing" to the difficult task of just *being*. He counsels elders to be patient and gentle—and to be *nothing*. A nursing-home resident rejected his advice, saying "What a lot of rot!" Returning two weeks later, however, he discovered that she had caught the message. She gave up worry, stopped fussing, and got the hang of doing nothing—and she was content.[10]

Even in the most limited circumstances, mentally challenged elders can experience joy in the present moment in ways that might seem infantile. Through the eyes of some onlookers, for example, the frail elderly woman gumming chocolate pudding—her face, fingers, and clothes smeared with the thick brown dessert—looks pathetic, even repulsive. Another observer is able to share vicariously the elder's experience of significant enjoyment in the texture and flavor of satisfying food, recognizing that this moment may indeed be experienced as an aesthetic delight giving as much satisfaction as a gourmet meal did in the past.[11] This, too, can be a religious experience, increasing joy and integrity in simple pleasures and helping one accept life as it unfolds, with gratitude.

The Role of Religious Institution

Religious institutions have the opportunity and responsibility to respond as resources allow to the spiritual needs of their members of all ages. Most of what is said of the church in the following illustration can apply to the synagogue and mosque as well. Consider the many needs of elders, both in ordinary times, as well as in times of crisis and at the hour of death, that can be met by a committed, faithful congregation.

In Ordinary Times

Religious community can preserve a sense of identity and self-esteem in the midst of the many changes and losses that come with increased age. The central biblical message is that

God loves all of humanity. Churches demonstrate the personal dignity of all people by valuing each of their members and by being inclusive communities.

Central to the ministry of the church is worship. Worship that is inclusive of different ages demonstrates the care for the dignity and loveableness of all. Elders can be enlisted as readers, liturgists, and from time to time preachers or dialogue partners with the pastor in delivering the sermon. Preaching and worship that emphasize God's unchanging love, the recitation of familiar Bible stories, and the singing of well-known hymns, the ongoing presence of caring people whose concern is unfaltering—all of these religious experiences offer comfort in a place that feels like home.

The Christian-education program of the church should include the educational needs of all generations, with elders sharing in the planning as well as the leadership. Churches have the resources to offer intergenerational opportunities for a variety of ongoing group experiences: Bible study, growth groups, study groups, prayer groups, and structured retreats. In my ideal congregation, all elders would be encouraged to participate in or lead a group of their choice.

In the area of pastoral care, elders could be trained by religious leaders to offer mutual spiritual friendship, care, and counsel to one another, as well as to younger members of the community. In some churches a team of seniors, organized and trained by a minister, carry on a thorough program of visitation, spending quality time with people in their homes, in hospitals, and in nursing homes. Visitation conveys that God is on the side of every one of God's people—both care givers and care receivers. An effective program of spiritual friendship and visitation increases the quality and quantity of love within the community. People know they are loved when others willingly and joyfully reach out to them. When people know that they have been gifted, loved, and served, they feel the need to give and love and serve in return.

In ordinary time, ministers of the church can be present to elders who are experiencing strong, troubling feelings like anger, guilt, or doubt—emotions mistakenly linked to sin. Elders can be helped to trust that their feelings are not only legitimate but profoundly human. When their anger or doubt is directed at God, people often feel guilty and blame themselves, making it difficult to forgive themselves or experience God's forgiveness. People convinced of the boundless love of God can help those trapped in guilt open themselves to God's mercy. Caring people who can be in the presence of pain, fear, and depression, without argument, without the need to rush in and provide answers, can meet the need of elders to express their true feelings and in many cases recover hope.

In Times of Crisis

The suffering side of aging—ill health, the death of partners and friends, and social isolation, test faith for all it is worth. People in crisis depend on the church; members of congregations often turn to their ministers first.

When a person or family is overwhelmed with serious medical problems and needs moral and spiritual support, the presence of a caregiver can provide soothing balm. While those in crisis must face the painful reality that confronts them, they also need to lift their minds and hearts above the immediate struggle. Through one-on-one conversation with a caregiver, through shared prayer, and at public worship, the one in crisis can seek the beyond, pray for perspective, hear the prayers offered, and be comforted both by the congregation and by the Holy One.

In Facing Death

Some elders and their families may struggle over the question of organ donation (an issue best raised long before critical illness). The donation of organs ought to be considered by all people of faith who recognize that they are coresponsible for one another. For Christians, belief in the Body of Christ might be sufficient motivation to share what one's body can no longer use with another whose body cannot be healed without it.

Others contend with serious ethical questions such as: Do I want to continue to live? Can I avoid pain? Will I be a burden on others? Will there be any money left for my survivors? Is it against God's will that I ease my way out of this life?

A full discussion of bioethics is beyond the scope of this book. People raising questions about euthanasia and life support need the attentive help of a wise and caring professional who is willing to listen deeply to the philosophical and religious beliefs of the questioner. Caregivers must be well grounded in their own ethical belief system and willing to share their convictions. Questions that might not surface outside such a safe and sensitive relationship are these: Of what value is my suffering life? Is God present to me at this time? Is my body holy ground? What is the most life-enhancing decision I can make at this time? How will my decision affect others?

These questions reveal my own difficulty with euthanasia. At the same time that I cannot assent to a person intentionally ending her or his life, I oppose keeping anyone alive by artificial means when there is little or no hope of their living a satisfying human life, and I favor keeping the terminally ill as pain free and comfortable as possible. Families and couples owe it to themselves to discuss the issue of medical treatment in detail long before they are confronted with a health crisis. They need to clarify through legal documents their wishes regarding life support and other decisions that may have to be made on their behalf.

Never is the question "How will I live until I die?" more critical than when a person knows that death is close at hand. Families quickly turn to people in ministry when death approaches. Assisting dying people and those they leave behind to communicate what needs to be said while there is yet time; helping survivors convey to their dying loved ones that it is all right for them to go; helping the terminally ill to say good-bye and die in peace—these are quintessential tasks of spiritual ministry.

In Gethsemane, Jesus made one of the few personal requests he ever made of his disciples. "I am deeply grieved, even to death; remain here, and stay awake with me" (Matthew 26:38). The seriously ill or dying may not say, "Stay awake and keep watch with me," but they need the assurance of human connection.

The Church as a Beacon for Intergenerational Life

Unlike any other social institution besides the extended family and in some unusual cases, neighborhoods, religious institutions can be examples of intergenerational life. In most religious institutions, participation in worship includes children, young adults, the middle-aged, and elders. Intergenerational worship, education programs, outreach, mentoring, growth groups, social engagement—all are possible. The people are in place, the location is secured, leadership is at hand, and time, talent, and economic resources are obtainable to make these happen.

Joel 2:28 provides the inspiration for a faith community to call on the gifts of all of its members: "I will pour out my spirit on all flesh; your sons and your daughters shall prophesy; your old men [and women] shall dream dreams, and your young men [and women] shall see visions." This is a view of intergenerational ministry: young and old, filled with the Spirit of God, bringing something new to life.

On stewardship Sunday in a local congregation, an elder and a young adult, a man and a woman perhaps fifty years apart in age, each spoke about the value of the church to their personal and family lives. That week the pastor, a member of the generation between the two speakers, had written to the congregation expressing the importance of the church in his extended family's life and his intention regarding his family's annual pledge. These three people of faith painted the picture of an effectively intergenerational church. Great efforts go into making the church's worship life, educational ministry, outreach, and time for retreat and recreation inclusive of all ages. The health of the congregation is in large part a result of its success in living intergenerationally.

Conclusion

While the values of elders are human values cherished by people of all ages, elders have a more pronounced interest in religious faith and participation in congregational life. One might wonder if religion is a matter of wishful thinking that props elders up so that they can endure. Those who are convinced that God is present here and now know in their heart of hearts that religion is rooted in reality. Why be surprised, they wonder, that it meets so many needs? Assessing, articulating, and pursuing one's needs and values can result in deeper satisfaction in the present, as one ages gracefully, generatively, and faithfully.

For Personal Reflection

1. Return to the value questions on pages 125–26. What cluster of values do you discern through your answers? Are these values evident in your present life? If not, what do you think gets in the way? Is there one value you would like to express more fully?

2. How might a close friend describe your values? You might check out your descriptions with this friend.

3. Review the major periods on the lifeline you constructed in chapter 4 and list the people who were most important to you at those times. After each name, include a few words that identify the gift you have given and the gift you have received in each relationship. In one case you may have given and received an enlarged sense of humor; in another, you may have instilled confidence and acquired a new sense of your power. Finally, go back over the list and write either the month and year when you were last in touch with each person, or the date of death if the person is no longer alive. What do you learn about yourself and these friends through this exercise?

4. Reflect on the ages of the people you consider to be friends. Are some at least a decade older, others a decade younger than you? If not, think of individuals in these age groups whom you might want to know better. How would you initiate contact with them?

5. How has religious faith functioned in your life? Are you involved in a faith community? If not, is such involvement something you would value?

Meditation

My heart is glad, and my soul rejoices. . . .
In your presence there is fullness of joy (Psalm 16:9,11).

Imagine yourself in a setting that evokes beauty and peace for you. Take time to notice the scene, returning to sights and sounds and smells that delight you. Take several deep breaths, enjoying the space you have created and relaxing as thoroughly as possible. Hear the words of the psalmist:

My heart is glad, and my soul rejoices. . . .
In your presence there is fullness of joy.

Breathing fresh air, sinking into quiet, deep comfort, prepare your mind and heart in hopeful expectation. Imagine with each breath you take that your heart expands and your imagination opens. You are ready for new ideas, renewed feelings of hope and joy. You are calm and quiet, at peace with yourself, happy to be alive, to be here, to be who you are today. Pray for inspiration. . . .

Reflect on what you most enjoy in your life today, and let gratitude fill your being. . . . With an attitude of playfulness and wonder, invite words or images that describe your values to bubble up in your consciousness. If one value clearly prevails at this time in your life, say the word or phrase quietly to yourself as you breathe in and out. . . .

My heart is glad, and my soul rejoices. . . .
In your presence there is fullness of joy.

Where does this value show up? Picture it in any form that your imagination offers. Can you put it to music? Does it dance? How do you celebrate this value? What more would you like to do with it? If names or faces you associate with this value come into your imagination, speak with these people about the values you are cherishing. What do you want to say? What do you want to hear?

Take time in bringing this reflection to a close, letting yourself be surprised and delighted by the value that is alive in you. Express what you most want to see happen in your present life. Close with the words:

My heart is glad, and my soul rejoices. . . .
In your presence there is fullness of joy.

Further Reflection

The questions and meditation undoubtedly reminded you of important people who have graced your life. Perhaps you have not been in touch with some of them; those relationships lie dormant. Choose one of these people and consider what steps you might take to bring this person up to date with your life journey and to discover what is happening in her or his life at this time.

7

Pulling It All Together

Older people have a particular responsibility to appreciate and nourish . . . diversity in age as well as in ethnic backgrounds. It is a great temptation to divest oneself of every responsibility possible in illness and age. That is not only a loss to the larger community but it may aggravate the illness and speed the aging of both soul and body.

—*Browne Barr,* Never Too Late To Be Loved

AS HE CALLED OUT THE NAMES of those whose seats would be given momentarily to stand-by passengers an airline agent shouted, "Snooze and lose!" To snooze one's way into old age is surely to lose out on new prospects. This chapter is a wake-up call as well as a conclusion. Each person stands at a crossroads. Losses and gains from the past, and future hopes and fears come together in the present moment, the only one that is fully available for realizing new possibilities. As a way of pulling together the work of this book, a final writing project reconsiders the past, the present, and the future.

The work of this book is about you, the reader. The reflections that you made and the insights you garnered while working through the book will coalesce in this brief final chapter in which you are asked to outline a story of your life. The work begins with a biblical reflection.

> Do not remember the former things,
>   or consider the things of old.
> I am about to do a new thing;
>   now it springs forth, do you not perceive it?
> I will make a way in the wilderness
>   and rivers in the desert (Isaiah 43:18-19).

In a guided meditation at a conference on retirement I used the words of Isaiah to encourage participants to explore the possibilities that lay before them at a major life transition. To acknowledge the life and lure of God alive in each person on each step of the journey, I shifted from "I am about to do a new thing" to "We are about to do a new thing." In the discussion that followed, a woman spoke of the discomfort she experienced when she heard "I am about to do a new thing." It felt as if something was about to be done to her, and she resisted. On the other hand, "We are about to do a new thing" sounded collaborative, exciting, comforting, inviting, and empowering.

To paraphrase Isaiah: "Do not remember the restrictions and hesitancies of old, the disappointments, failures, and discouragement. We are about to do a new thing. Pay attention. Now it springs forth. Do you not perceive it? There are both footpaths and springs of water in what may look like wilderness and desert." Old age is freedom for something new.

Reflective Pause

What will be new for you? In a meditative state, prayerfully read both the biblical passages and the paraphrase, hearing the words addressed to you.

Waking Up to New Possibilities

"Waking Up to New Possibilities" encourages you to look thoughtfully, kindly, and courageously at your life as a whole.[1] You might choose where to focus additional energies in order to enjoy more faithful aging. For some the work will continue the looking back begun in chapter 4; others will focus on the present; still others will attend to the future. Keeping the words of Isaiah in mind, remember that whichever way you search, you are not alone in bringing a new thing into being. Perhaps your work will entail more reflecting, remembering, and reliving than putting thoughts on paper. Remember that you need only an outline. Some readers, however, may choose to write a full narrative. Here is an outline, followed by clarifications and comments about its details.

Waking Up to New Possibilities
A Story of Your Life

Author

Title (Leave the title blank until the end.)

1. Reclaiming a usable past
   Genogram of your nuclear family
   Core family values
   Core family narrative
   Coming of age
   First adult dream
   Midlife dream
   Turning point(s)
   Wake-up calls

2. Taking stock of the present

If you believe you are in transition, describe the transition—from what to what or where to where?

What do you most value about your life now?

What concerns do you have about your life at the present time?

3. Moving into the future

How would you describe your future story?

What title would you like to give the next phase of your life?

Are you aware of unlived life seeking your attention?

Explanation of the Outline

A *genogram* is a three-generational family diagram or family tree that charts the names of family members with their births, dates of marriages or holy unions, and deaths. Unrelated children and adults who lived with the family are included. Your diagram provides a symbolic snapshot of the people who influenced your early life as well as the makeup of your present family.[2]

Core family values and the core family narrative were discussed in chapter 4. Conversation with parents, siblings, and family friends can help you pinpoint the "party line" or themes in the *narrative.*

Coming of age asks that you recapture your experience of moving from childhood to adult consciousness. You might still have been a child or adolescent when life circumstances propelled you into adult consciousness, namely, when you were forced to face the reality of human limitations or when you suffered the abuse of power: loss, illness, or death in the family; physical or emotional abuse, incest or rape. If you were blessed by being nurtured in a nonabusive family, your coming of age would be quite different. How do you describe your moment of coming of age? What challenge entered your life at that time?

Return to your *first adult dream*. How did you hope your adulthood would unfold? Consider subsequent turning points in your life. What did you turn from? What did you turn toward?

Wake-up calls are breakthrough moments when you are confronted with reality; they tend to pivot around awareness of age and of the brevity of life. Wake-up calls that are heard result in a person taking a step in a new direction.

Next, *take stock of the present*, considering your current values and concerns. Finally, *speculate on the future*, briefly describing what you want to see happen in the next phase of your life. The final task in this exercise is to come up with a *title* that best describes the story of your life. The next steps are yours as you respond to the call to faithful aging.

Conclusion

Most people find beginnings much easier than endings, which is not surprising given the human resistance to face limits and readiness to deny death. Every ending is an intimation of the final end. Many people avoid saying good-bye, resist bringing projects to a conclusion, in a hurry to move on to the next thing rather than intentionally reaching closure.

At the opening session of a semester, I bound into a classroom loaded with syllabi, books, ideas, and expectations, my faith and hope high, my heart excited over the new thing that is ready for birth. A fresh team of people is about to make a covenant to learn something together and to do it with care and kindness. Excitement is in the air. The last day of class, which always includes a wrap-up and evaluation, has a solemn feel to it. The new thing is coming to an end, a part of the past rather than the present. Finding the words to say good-bye and move on is difficult.

The Art of Growing Old has gone through a parallel process. I was eager to write the introduction. It wrote itself in my imagination and flew from my eager finger-tips onto the screen, challenging me line by line. Con-cluding is a different matter. "Faithful Aging" has become more than a phrase to me. I cherish the reading I have done, the conversations I have enjoyed, and the relation-ship that developed with the ideas that became a book, a relationship that strangely includes readers who do not yet exist, and when they do come into being will remain mostly strangers to me and to one another. The work started here does not end, however, as long as there are opportunities to wake up and turn possibilities into actualities.

I am at the beginning of faithful aging. Perhaps the most exciting realization has been increased freshness in my own faith in the ancient God who is constantly reborn and is ever so active in the challenging lives of faithful elders. I appreciate with renewed faith a Trinitarian God who is always *we* and an incarnate God who brings flesh to that partnership. I know as I may not have known before that ultimately all relationship, all value, all renew-al, the gain beyond all loss, rests in God, the source of all possibility, the only one whose life is not bounded by death. In my present moment I reach out in faith to the one whose present moment is an eternal now. Now is the time to let go of the beginning and move further into the challenge.

Thank you for joining the conversation that has not yet happened. I hope our paths cross.

Appendix A

Group Study

WHAT SHOULD BE THE MAKEUP OF A group addressing faithful aging? The group could be intergenerational—faith communities offer an excellent opportunity for such membership. Or, it could be made up of people of about the same age, who share similar historical and social-world backgrounds. There are advantages and disadvantages to both options.

An intergenerational group represents life at its many stages; all members of any group are obviously aging. Increased knowledge and understanding of how people face personal and social challenges at various points in the life cycle is a clear advantage of a mixed-age group. Older people who feel isolated from the younger generations might most welcome this opportunity. Young people who do not have frequent occasion to interact with their elders would also gain from being in an intergenerational group. Another benefit is that when group members are at various stages of life, those people with very different ideas or values do not create the same pressure or pose the same threat to them as someone their own age might. There is no need to conform to a different age group's choices. For example, if one after another friend in my age group becomes convinced that only a low-fat diet makes good sense I will feel pressure to change my high-fat eating habits. If the people moving toward low-fat foods are twenty years older or younger than myself, I may not feel the same pressure to change.

Elders born within the same decade, on the other hand, might more easily reclaim a usable past together. Growing up with relatively the same "ground rules" and cultural experiences allows for mutual understanding that enriches the past, making it more usable. The success of such a group was illustrated by seventy-five-year-old men who spent prolonged time together living as if they were fifty-five.

Once the age question is resolved, the issue of gender must be faced. Should the group be for women only, men only, or both? Obviously there are advantages to each of these options. Each community would have to assess its needs and desires with regard to establishing groups to foster faithful aging.

Appendix B

Facilitating Guided Meditations

THE SPACE USED FOR THE MEDITATION should be quiet, attractive, and comfortable. The use of candles, soft lights, and art objects can enhance the experience.

The facilitator allows ten to fifteen minutes for the meditation and another ten to fifteen minutes for debriefing. The facilitator explains that in a guided meditation, certain details will be suggested, and participants then let their imaginations take over. If their mind wanders, they might gently come back to the proposed scene and pick up with the meditation. Those who are comfortable closing their eyes might have fewer distractions.

Participants are advised to sit straight in their chairs, make themselves as comfortable as possible, relax, then take several deep breaths, slowly inhaling and exhaling. This is a time of calming, quieting, gently setting aside distractions, and letting outside noises be.

The facilitator might say a few times, "You are becoming relaxed, letting stress go. You are present to yourself," perhaps adding phrases such as "more deeply relaxed" or "centered and peaceful," and providing several moments of silence. The dots in the meditation designate pauses in the reading.

After the meditation the facilitator counts down from ten to one very slowly. Following a minute or two of silence as participants return to this time and space, group members could be asked to share with one other person whatever they feel comfortable sharing from the meditation. A general discussion follows.

Appendix C

Resources

American Association of Homes Services for the Aging
901 E Street N.W., Suite 500
Washington, D.C. 20004

American Association of Retired People (AARP)
1901 K Street N.W.
Washington, D.C. 20049

Gray Panthers
P.O. Box 21477
Washington, D.C. 20009 or
2025 Pennsylvania Avenue S.W.
Washington, D.C. 20077-2668

National Association of State Units on Aging
2033 K Street N.W., Suite 304
Washington, D.C. 20006

National Council on the Aging
409 Third Street S.W.
Washington, D.C. 20024

National Interfaith Coalition on Aging
409 Third Street S.W.
Washington, D.C. 20024

Older Women's League
666 11th Street N.W. #700
Washington, D.C. 20001-4512

Retired Senior Volunteer Program (RSVP)
5492 La Sierra
Dallas, Tex. 75231

Notes

Introduction

1. De Bernieres 1994, 402–403.

2. This moment of recognition eventuated in my writing my own definition of ageism. Ageism is the disvaluing of a person or group because of their chronological age; it is an inability or unwillingness to see oneself or accept oneself as an aging person.

3. Bureau of the Census Statistical Brief, May 1995

4. Adler 1995, 10

5. For an excellent essay on the importance of remaining active in old age, see Paul Tournier, "Lifestyles Leading to Physical, Mental and Social Wellbeing in Old Age" in Clements 1988, 13–26.

6. Neugarten 1968, 171–72

7. Atchley 1989, 183–84

8. Shock et al. 1984, 207; McCrae and Costa 1982, 301; National Institute of Aging, 1989

9. Bednar, Wells, and Peterson 1989

Chapter 1

1. Blythe 1979, 94

2. Snorton 1996, 57

3. Harris 1995

4. Blythe 1979, 96

5. At the time Alzheimer's Disease was not broadly discussed. The word *senility* covered varieties of loss of short-term memory, and people in Granny's world knew that she was senile. Alzheimer's Disease is one of two primary causes of dementia—the other is multi-infarct dementia. Beck and Pearson 1989, 187

6. Carr 1988, 57

7. Maslow 1962

Chapter 2

1. Mitchell and Anderson 1983, 46–51

2. "Network loss" is a term used by Maria Tecala of the Center for Loss and Grief Therapy in Kensington, Maryland. I am indebted to Kenneth Mitchell and Herbert Anderson for their insightful overview of loss in human life. See *All Our Losses, All Our Griefs* 1983, 35–52.

3. For a picture of the grim economic and health situation of old persons throughout the world, and especially of poor women, see Paul and Paul, 1994.

4. Pearson and Beck 1989, 152–60

5. Pogribin 1996, 100–01

6. Narayan and Quinn 1996, 5

7. Seaver 1994

8. Another source reports that only 2 percent of people aged 65–74 in this country are institutionalized; 7 percent of those 75–84; 20 percent of those 85 and older. People aged 65 have between a 25 percent and 40 percent chance of spending some time in a nursing home during their remaining years. Garner and Mercer 1989, 26.

9. Koenig 1994, 353, 403

10. Devons 1996; Rice 1989, 248

11. Murphy 1996, 13; Beck and Pearson 1989, 186

12. Pruyser 1975, 108
13. Seymour 1995, 23
14. Payne 1990, 31
15. Cited in Sullender, 1989, 95. Robert J. Havinghurst and Eugene A. Friedmann. 1954. *The Meaning of Work and Retirement*, Chicago: University of Chicago Press.

Chapter 3

1. Stock 1995
2. Blythe 1979, 124
3. Stock 1995
4. Blythe 1979, 13, 16
5. Payne and McFadden 1994, 16
6. Scott-Maxwell 1968, 13, 142
7. Kuhn 1980, 202–203
8. Seaver 1994
9. Butler 1975, 263
10. Halamandaris 1991
11. Robb 1991, ix
12. Dasher 1996, 181
13. Swenson 1994, 81
14. Bureau of the Census 1995
15. Lang 1993, 30–31
16. Sarton 1993, 41
17. Goldman and Mahler 1995, 184
18. Weeks and James 1995
19. Taylor 1987, 25–26
20. Maccallum 1990, 6, 11–12
21. Halamandaris 1991, 28
22. Hessel 1977, 91–92
23. Goldman 1995, 5–11
24. Carter 1993

Chapter 4

1. Pogrebin 1996, 120

2. Subsequent research has refuted Butler, demonstrating that future story is neither peculiar to elders nor universal among them. Molinari and Reichlin 1985, 90.

3. Pogrebin 1966, 121

4. Incorporated in these exercises are ideas from Richard Morgan 1995, and James Birren and Donna Deutchman 1991 on the lifeline exercise and Ira Progoff's 1975 methods in the dialogue section.

Chapter 5

1. Lester 1995, 74–82

2. Pacheco 1989, 10–11

3. Rosen 1982, 167–70

4. Questions are based on Hudson and McLean 1995, 83

Chapter 6

1. I borrow the notion of the bunch of grapes from Carol Tavris 1989, who says that emotions are not particularly distinctive. They cluster like bunches of grapes.

2. Raths, Harmin and Simon 1966

3. Sarton 1996, 1980

4. Adler 1995, 133–36

5. Nouwen 1981, 295

6. Manheimer 1994, 348, 352–53

7. Koenig 1995, 12–13

8. Koenig 1994, 178, 184; 1995, 14–15, 24

9. Moberg 1968, 504–508; 1994, 546

10. Blythe 1979, 306

11. Jackson 1981, 81

Chapter 7

1. An exercise presented by family therapist Carol Anderson at the Family Networker conference in Washington, D.C. 1995 inspired the flow of this book. Anderson's theme was "wake-up calls," moments of truth that alert the middle-aged that life is moving on. "Waking Up to New Possibilities" is an adaptation of the handout she used at the workshop.

2. See Monica McGoldrick and Randy Gerson, *Genograms in Family Assessment.* New York: W. W. Norton, 1985 for a full discussion of genograms.

Bibliography

Adler, Lynn Peters. 1995. *Centenarians: The Bonus Years.* Health Press.

Atchley, Robert. 1989. "A Continuity Theory of Normal Aging." *Gerontologist* 29, 2: 183–90.

Axline, Virginia. 1964. *Dibs In Search of Self.* New York: Ballantine.

Barr, Browne. 1996. *Never Too Late To Be Loved: How One Couple Under Stress Discovered Intimacy and Joy.* Shippensburg, Pa.: Ragged Edge Press.

Beck, Cornelia M. and Pearson, Barbara P. 1989. "Mental Health of Elderly Women." In Garner and Mercer, 175–93.

Becker, Ernest. 1974. *The Denial of Death.* New York: Free Press.

Bednar, Richard L.; Wells, M. Gawain; and Peterson, Scott R. 1989. *Self-Esteem: Paradoxes and Innovations in Clinical Theory and Practice.* Washington, D.C.: American Psychological Association.

Bianchi, Eugene C. 1982. *Aging as a Spiritual Journey.* New York: Crossroad.

Bianchi, Eugene C. 1985. *On Growing Older: A Personal Guide to Life after Thirty-five.* New York: Crossroad.

Bianchi, Eugene C. 1994. *Elder Wisdom: Crafting Your Own Elderhood.* New York: Crossroad.

Birren, James E. 1993. "Understanding Life Backwards: Reminiscing for a Better Old Age." In Butler and Kiikuni, 18–29.

Birren, James E. and Deutchman, Donna E. 1991. *Guiding Autobiography Groups for Older Adults: Exploring the Fabric of Life*. Baltimore: Johns Hopkins University Press.

Blythe, Ronald. 1979. *The View in Winter: Reflections on Old Age*. London: Allen Lane, Penguin Books, Ltd.

Buford, Paula. 1996. "Women and Community: Women's Study Groups as Pastoral Counseling." In Moessner, 285–303.

Butler, Robert N. 1963. "The Life Review: An Interpretation of Reminiscence in the Aged." *Psychiatry* 26: 65–76.

Butler, Robert N. 1975. *Why Survive? Being Old in America*. New York: Harper and Row.

Butler, Robert N. and Kenso, Kiikuni, eds. 1993. *Who Is Responsible for My Old Age?* New York: Springer.

Caldwell, Cleopatra Howard; Chatters, Linda M.; Billingsley, Andrew; and Taylor, Robert Joseph. 1995. "Church-Based Support Programs for Elderly Black Adults: Congregational and Clergy Characteristics." In Kimble et al., 306–24.

Carlsen, Mary Baird. 1991. *Creative Aging: A Meaning-Making Perspective*. New York: W. W. Norton.

Carr, Anne. 1988. *A Search for Wisdom and Spirit: Thomas Merton's Theology of the Self*. South Bend, Ind.: University of Notre Dame Press.

Carter, Stephen L. 1993. *The Culture of Disbelief: How American Law and Politics Trivialize Religious Devotion*. New York: Basic Books.

Clements, William M. 1990. "Religious Development in the Fourth Quarter of Life," *Journal of Religious Gerontology* 7: 55–70.

Clements, William M., ed. 1988. *Religion, Aging and Health: A Global Perspective*. New York: Haworth Press.

Coles, Robert. 1973. *The Old Ones of New Mexico.* Albu-
querque: University of New Mexico Press.

Collins, P. H. 1990. *Black Feminist Thought: Knowledge, Consciousness and the Politics of Empowerment.* Boston:
Unwin Hyman.

Copper, Baba. 1988. *Over the Hill: Reflections on Ageism
Between Women.* Freedom, Calif.: The Crossing Press.

Dasher, Jane E. 1996. "Manna in the Desert: Eating Disor-
ders and Pastoral Care." In Moessner, 179–91.

De Bernieres, Louis. 1994. *Corelli's Mandolin.* New York:
Vintage Books.

Devons, Cathryn A. J. 1996. "Suicide in the Elderly: How to
Identify and Treat Patients at Risk." *Geriatrics* 51, 67–72.

Downes, Peggy; Tuttle, Ilene; Faul, Patricia; and Mudd, Virginia. 1996. *The New Older Woman: A Dialogue for the
Coming Century.* Berkeley: Celestial Arts.

Dulin, Rachel Z. 1988. *A Crown of Glory: A Biblical View of
Aging.* New York: Paulist Press.

Erikson, Erik H. 1950. *Childhood and Society.* New York:
W. W. Norton.

Friedan, Betty. 1993. "Beyond the Mystique of Old Age." In
Butler and Kenso, 57–72.

Garner, J. Dianne and Mercer, Susan O., eds. 1989. *Women As
They Age: Challenge, Opportunity, and Triumph.* New
York: Haworth Press.

Geddes, Donald Porter. 1945. *Franklin Delano Roosevelt: A
Memorial.* Montreal, Canada: Pocket Books.

Goldman, Connie and Mahler, Richard. 1995. *Secrets of
Becoming a Late Bloomer: Extraordinary Ordinary People
on the Art of Staying Creative, Alive, and Aware in Mid-Life
and Beyond.* Walpole, N.H.: Stillpoint.

Gottlieb, Naomi. 1989. "Families, Work, and the Lives of
Older Women." In Garner and Mercer, 217–44.

Grauman, Brigid. 1995. "Happy, Healthy and Odd: Nonconformists Live Longer." *The Wall Street Journal,* November 2, 1995, Leisure and Arts, A16.

Halamandaris, Val J. 1991. *Profiles in Caring: Advocates for the Elderly.* Washington, D.C.: Caring Publishing.

Harris, Louis. 1974. "Who the Senior Citizens Really Are." In LeFevre and LeFevre 1981, 117–22.

Harris, Maria. 1995. *Jubilee Time: Celebrating Women, Spirit, and the Advent of Age.* New York: Bantam Books.

Havinghurst, Robert J., Neugarten, Bernice L. and Tobin, Sheldon S., "Disengagement and Patterns of Aging." In Neugarten, 161–77.

Hessel, Dieter, ed. 1977. *Maggie Kuhn on Aging: A Dialogue.* Philadelphia: Westminster.

Hiltner, Seward, ed. 1975. *Toward a Theology of Aging,* special issue of *Pastoral Psychology.* New York: Human Sciences Press.

Hiltner, Seward. 1981. "A Theology of Aging." in LeFevre, and LeFevre, 45–55.

Hubbs-Tait, Laura. 1989. "Coping Patterns of Aging Women: A Developmental Perspective." In Garner and Mercer, 95–121.

Hudson, Frederic M. and McLean, Pamela D. 1995. *Life Launch: A Passionate Guide to the Rest of Your Life.* Santa Barbara, Calif.: The Hudson Institute Press.

Jackson, Gordon E. 1981. *Pastoral Care and Process Theology.* Lanham, Md.: University Press of America.

Justes, Emma. 1996. "Pastoral Care and Older Women's Secrets." In Moessner, 240–53.

Karp, David A. 1988. "A Decade of Reminders: Changing Age Consciousness Between Fifty and Sixty Years Old." *Gerontologist* 28,6: 727–38.

Kimble, Melvin A.; McFadden, Susan H.; Ellor, James W.; and Seeber, James J., eds. 1995. *Aging, Spirituality, and*

Religion: A Handbook. Minneapolis: Fortress Press.

Knudson, Mary. 1995. "A Feminist Theology of Aging." In Kimble et al., 460–82.

Koenig, Harold G. 1994. *Aging and God: Spiritual Pathways to Mental Health in Midlife and Later Years*. New York: Haworth Pastoral Press.

Koenig, Harold G. 1995. "Religion and Health in Later Life." In Kimble et al., 9–29.

Kübler-Ross, Elisabeth. 1969. *On Death and Dying*. New York: Macmillan Co.

Kuhn, Margaret S. 1980. "Spiritual Well-Being as a Celebration of Wholeness." In Thorson and Cook, 201–204.

Lang, Eugene M. 1993. "We Have a Dream: The Generations Working Together Toward the Future." In Butler and Kiikuni, 33–39.

Langer, Ellen J. 1989. *Mindfulness*. Reading, Mass.: Addison-Wesley.

LeFevre, Carol and Perry, eds. 1981. *Aging and the Human Spirit: A Reader in Religion and Gerontology*. Chicago: Exploration Press.

Lester, Andrew. 1995. *Hope in Pastoral Care and Counseling*. Louisville: Westminster John Knox Press.

Maccallum, Donald J. 1990. "Aging Congregations and the Divinity School." Unpublished Doctor of Ministry thesis, Yale Divinity School.

Macdonald, Barbara with Rich, Cynthia. 1983. *Look Me In the Eye: Old Women, Aging and Ageism*. San Francisco: Spinsters Ink.

Maddox, George L., ed. 1995. *The Encyclopedia of Aging*. 2nd ed. New York: Springer.

Manheimer, Ronald J., ed. 1994. *Older Americans Almanac: A Reference Work on Seniors in the United States*. Washington, D.C.: Gale Research.

Maslow, Abraham H. 1962. *Toward a Psychology of Being*.

Princeton: Van Nostrand.

Maslow, Abraham H. 1964. *Religions, Values and Peak Experiences.* Columbus, Ohio: Ohio University Press.

Maslow, Abraham H. 1971. *The Farther Reaches of Human Nature.* New York: Viking Press.

McCrae, Robert R. and Costa, Paul T. 1982. "Aging, the Life Course, and Models of Personality," in Shock 1984, 292–303 (reprinted from Field, T. M.; Houston, A.; Quay, H. C.; Troll, L; Finley, G. E.; editors, *Review of Human Development.* New York: Wiley.)

Merriam, Sharan B.; Martin, Peter; Adkins, Geneva; and Poon, Leonard. 1995. "Centenarians: Their Memories and Future Ambitions." *International Journal of Aging and Human Development,* 41(2) 117–32.

Mitchell, Kenneth and Anderson, Herbert. 1983. *All Our Losses, All Our Griefs.* Philadelphia: Westminster.

Moberg, David O. 1968. "Religiosity in Old Age." In Neugarten, 497–508.

Moberg, David O. 1995. "Applications of Research Methods." In Kimble et al., 541–57.

Moessner, Jeanne Stevenson, ed. 1996. *Through the Eyes of Women: Insights for Pastoral Care.* Minneapolis: Fortress Press.

Molinari, Victor and Reichlin, Robert E. 1985. "Reminiscence in the Elderly: A Review of the Literature" *International Journal of Aging and Human Development* 20,2: 81–92.

Moody, Harry R. 1995. "Mysticism." In Kimble et al., 87-101.

Morgan, Richard L. 1995. "Guiding Spiritual Autobiography Groups for Third and Fourth Agers." *Journal of Religious Gerontology* 9:1-14.

Murphy, Caryle. 1996. "Suicide by Elderly Called Avoidable." *The Washington Post.* August 6, Health, 13.

Narayan, Sanjiv and Quinn, Bruce. 1996. "The Aging of the

Brain, The Aging of the Mind: A Seminar for Health Professionals." Stanford, Calif.: The CorTexT Institute.

National Institute of Aging. 1989. *Older and Wiser: The Baltimore Longitudinal Study of Aging.*

Neugarten, Bernice ed. 1968. *Middle Age and Aging: A Reader in Social Psychology.* Chicago: University of Chicago Press.

Nouwen, Henri J. J. 1981. "Care for the Elderly." In LeFevre and LeFevre, 291–96.

Ornish, Dean. 1993. *Eat More, Weigh Less.* New York: Harper Collins.

Pacheco, Catherine Chapman. 1989. *Breaking Patterns: Redesigning Your Later Years.* New York: Andrews and McMeel.

Payne, Barbara Pittard and McFadden, Susan H. 1994. "From Loneliness to Solitude: Religious and Spiritual Journeys in Late Life." In Thomas and Eisenhandler, 3–27.

Payne, Barbara. 1990. "Spiritual Maturity and Meaning-Filled Relationships: A Sociological Perspective." *Journal of Religious Gerontology* 7: 25–39.

Pearson, Barbara P. and Beck, Cornelia M. 1989. "Physical Health of Elderly Women." In Garner and Mercer, 149–74.

Pogrebin, Letty Cottin. 1996. *Getting Over Getting Older: An Intimate Journey.* New York: Little, Brown and Co.

Progoff, Ira. 1975. *At a Journal Workshop: The Basic Text and Guide for Using the Intensive Journal.* New York: Dialogue House.

Pruyser, Paul W. 1975. "Aging: Downward, Upward, or Forward?" In Hiltner 1975, 102–18.

Raths, Louis E.; Harmin, Merrill; and Simon, Sydney B. 1966. *Values and Teaching: Working with Values in the Classroom.* Columbus, Ohio: Charles E. Merrill.

Rice, Susan. 1989. "Sexuality and Intimacy for Aging

Women: A Changing Perspective." In Garner and Mercer, 245–64.

Rico, Gabriele Lusser. 1983. *Writing the Natural Way*. Los Angeles: Jeremy P. Tarcher.

Robb, Thomas B. 1991. *Growing Up: Pastoral Nurture for the Later Years*. New York: Haworth Press.

Rokeach, Milton. 1973. *The Nature of Human Values*. New York: Free Press.

Rosen, Sidney, ed. 1982. *My Voice Will Go with You: The Teaching Tales of Milton H. Erickson*. New York: W. W. Norton.

Sarton, May. 1980. *Recovering: A Journal*. New York: W. W. Norton.

Sarton, May. 1988. *After the Stroke: A Journal*. New York: W. W. Norton.

Sarton, May. 1993. *Encore: A Journal of the Eightieth Year*. New York: W. W. Norton.

Sarton, May. 1996. *At Eighty–Two: A Journal*. New York: W. W. Norton.

Saussy, Carroll. 1991. *God Images and Self–Esteem: Empowering Women in a Patriarchal Society*. Louisville: Westminster John Knox Press.

Saussy, Carroll. 1995. *The Gift of Anger: A Call to Faithful Action*. Louisville: Westminster John Knox Press.

Scott-Maxwell, Florida. 1968. *The Measure of My Days*, New York: Alfred Knopf.

Seaver, A. M. H. 1994. "My World Now: Life in a Nursing Home, From the Inside." *Newsweek*, "My Turn," June 27, 1994, 11.

Seeber, James J., ed. 1990. *Spiritual Maturity in the Later Years*. New York: Haworth Press.

Seymour, Robert E. 1995. *Aging without Apology: Living the Senior Years with Integrity and Faith*. Valley Forge, Pa.: Judson Press.

Sheehy, Gail. 1976. *Passages: Predictable Crises of Adult Life.* New York: Bantam.

Sheehy, Gail. 1995. *New Passages: Mapping Your Life Across Time.* New York: Random House.

Shock, Nathan W.; Greulich, Richard C.; Andres, Reubin; Arenberg, David; Costa, Paul T. Jr.; Lakatta, Edward G.; and Tobin, Jordan D. 1984. *Normal Human Aging: The Baltimore Longitudinal Study of Aging.* NIH publication #84-2450. Washington, D. C.: U.S. Department of Health and Human Services.

Snorton, Teresa E. 1996. "The Legacy of the African-American Matriarch: New Perspectives for Pastoral Care. In Moessner, 50–65.

Stock, Robert. 1995. "Senior Class." *The New York Times,* Home Section, June 1, 1995.

Sullender, R. Scott. 1989. *Losses In Later Life: A New Way of Walking with God.* New York: Paulist Press.

Swenson, Harriet Kerr. 1994. *Visible & Vital: A Handbook for the Aging Congregation.* New York: Paulist Press.

Tavris, Carol. 1989. *Anger: The Misunderstood Emotion.* New York: Simon & Schuster.

Taylor, Blaine. 1987. *The Church's Ministry with Older Adults.* Nashville: Abingdon Press.

Thibault, Jane. 1995. "Congregation as a Spiritual Care Community." In Kimble et al. 350–61.

Thomas, L. Eugene and Eisenhandler, Susan A., eds. 1994. *Aging and the Religious Dimension.* Westport, Conn.: Greenwood.

Thorson, James A. 1995. *Aging in a Changing Society.* Washington, D.C.: Wadsworth Publishing Company.

Thorson, James A. and Cook, Thomas C. 1980. *Spiritual Well-Being of the Elderly.* Springfield, Ill: Charles C. Thomas.

Tournier, Paul. 1988. "Lifestyles Leading to Physical, Mental and Social Wellbeing in Old Age." In Clements 1988, 13–26.

Trafford, Abigail. 1996. "Growing Old is Largely a Job for Women." *The Washington Post*. January 16, Health, 6.

Viorst, Judith. 1986. *Necessary Losses: The Loves, Illusions, Dependencies and Impossible Expectations That All of Us Have to Give Up in Order to Grow*. New York: Fawcett Gold Medal.

Walker, Barbara G. 1985. *The Crone: Woman of Age, Wisdom, and Power*. San Francisco: Harper & Row.

Weeks, David, and James, Jamie. 1995. *Eccentrics: A Study of Sanity and Strangeness*. New York: Villard Books.

Wilber Cross. 1991. *The Henry Holt Retirement Sourcebook: An Information Guide for Planning and Managing Your Affairs*. New York: Henry Holt & Co.

Williams, Wendy Swallow. 1996. "50 Things to Do Before I Die." *The Washington Post*. July 4, Style Plus, C5.

Printed in the United States
91178LV00002B/226/A